Helen Dykema Dengler

Del Rio, Texas, U.S.A.

January 25, 2002

White Sun's creators, Jack and Helen Dengler, made music an integral part of the ranch. Singing "In München steht ein Hofbrauhäus," they welcome guests to the Oktoberfest Reunion, October 13, 1962.

WHITE SUN

MEMOIRS OF A DESERT GUEST RANCH

BY

HELEN DYKEMA DENGLER

EDITED BY

NANCY DENGLER STARBUCK

GATEWAY PRESS, INC.
Baltimore, MD   2002

ENDSHEETS:
Aerial view of the White Sun Guest Ranch in 1966.

United Aerial Survey Photo

Please direct all correspondence and book orders to:
Helen Dykema Dengler
119 Pauline Ave
Del Rio, TX 78840

Library of Congress Control Number 2001 135369

Cover design by Nancy Starbuck

Published for the author by
Gateway Press, Inc.
1001 N. Calvert Street
Baltimore, MD 21202-3897

Printed in the United States of America

For Jack

"The real desert is not for the eyes of the superficial observer, nor the fearful soul or the cynic. It is a land whose character is hidden except to those who come with friendliness and understanding. To these the desert offers rare gifts: health-giving sunshine, a night sky that is studded with diamonds, a breeze that bears no poison, a landscape of pastel colors such as no artist can duplicate, thorn-covered plants which during countless ages have clung tenaciously to life through heat and drought and wind and the depredations of thirsty animals, and yet each season send forth blossoms of exquisite coloring as a symbol of courage that has triumphed over terrifying obstacles."

—Randall Henderson

Contents

Foreword

I was not prepared for shocking news, when the phone rang at our Texas home on Monday, November 25, 1991. A reporter was on the line from the Palm Springs newspaper, THE DESERT SUN. He wanted some background information on WHITE SUN GUEST RANCH, which had burned to the ground that same day.[1]

For Jack this news was not all that disquieting. He had begun building the ranch in 1946 right after the war. For the next thirty-three years he kept developing and improving what became a world renowned, highly successful guest ranch. For him White Sun lost its challenge once that goal had been achieved, and in 1979, Jack decided to sell the ranch and move on.

He told the reporter, "I've just turned my back on it once and for all. But yes, it will hurt a little."

For me that news hurt a lot. My struggle to accept and appreciate the complexities of life in the desert, which at first had seemed so threatening and hostile, had come full circle. During my years at the ranch I learned to love the place and to understand how enormous the challenge was becoming to preserve this fragile desert. Accepting Jack's decision to sell the ranch and relocate in Texas had been very difficult.

Remembering all our struggles, the creativity, the planning, the place we raised our six children and made such a host of wonderful, new friends, should all this history suddenly disappear in flames? True enough, White Sun ceased to be our responsibility when new owners took over in 1979. Yet twelve years later, regardless of whether it was an act of vandalism or just the inevitability of new development, the burning of White Sun was all the incentive I needed to tell its story.

Acknowledgments

White Sun, as I knew it in the 20th Century, has disappeared without a trace. But not so in the hearts of former guests and staff, whom I was fortunate to locate and who generously shared their recollections with me. Among those very much alive White Sunners, I am indebted to Topsy and Forry Haller, our first ranch managers, and to our last, True Slocum Taft and Kathy Williams.

Special kudos to our promotional genius, Janet Farrington Rouse, as well as my office staffers, resourceful "Girl Friday" Lynn Morgan, Betty Ring Shelton, Kathy Maclean Ferguson, and Nancy Carruthers Rorty.

More bravos to extraordinary chef Jean Schaffer, who wore two hats working for White Sun and SITA World Travel, as did Marianne Bohn Szymanski, Birthe Andersen Bang, and Sue Hey.

Vivid flashbacks were provided by Marge Anderson, Louella Fincher, "B" Bennett, Ed Burton, Deedee Bennett Busch, Betty Upton Gates, Mary Garton Jarrell, Shirley P. Jones, Armin Lehmann, Nancy Levensaler, and Inder Sharma.

I thank my six children for their contributions and steadfast support: my editor, Nancy Dengler Starbuck, sleuth, poet, B&B entrepreneur, mother of Orca and Rachel Starbuck.

Ian Cargan Dengler, historian, logician, swimmer, president and soul (!) member of the UNIVERSITAS CANUS RUFFUS (University of Barkology), Sic Canus Ruffit Quaere. Ian always reminded me, "When in doubt, put it in."

David Barry Dengler, microbiologist, medical/technologist, former SITA manager and tour leader, birder, keen observer of the natural world. David owned the first (Ramzar I) of many Dengler Chocolate Labradors.

Roger Mark Dengler, world traveler, skilled craftsman, musician, computer whiz, e-Business Operations Manager for ION SYSTEMS. Mark affectionately recalled our Swiss gentlemen neighbor, Walter Troesch, who became the ultimate desert hermit, homesteading in the middle of the worst sand-blow area, but fit as a fiddle.

Lorinda Ann Dengler, PhD professor of Geology at Humboldt State University, lecturer, tsunami and world earthquake authority, mother of Karl, Peter, and Clara Lisle. Lori, with Gale Levensaler, originated White Sun's popular Easter Horse Show.

Lissa Dengler Wheeler, composer, pianist, singer, cranial sacral technician, Integrated Manual Therapy instructor both in the U.S. and abroad, and currently a PhD candidate at the University of Westbrook.

Vital research data came from Mrs. Harriet Allen of the Desert Protective Council; biologist Lloyd Tevis and Nona; Pete Dangermond of the Dangermond Group; Dave Heveron of The Living Desert, and Karen Sausman, Executive Director of The Living Desert; Dr. John L. Norman and geologist Harry Quinn of College of The Desert; Chambers of Commerce in Palm Desert, Palm Springs and Rancho Mirage; Palm Desert Historical Society; Palm Springs Desert Museum's Jim Cornett and George Meyer; Palm Springs Historical Society; The Village Green Heritage Center; the Santa Rosa Visitors Center; my Texas Congressman, The Honorable Henry Bonilla, and the U.S. Forest Services' Skip Benediktson.

Bouquets to Shelley Croft and Andrea McKinley of Insty Prints in Polson, Montana.

Nancy Carrol Tarry Benediktson again took on the crucial job of proofreading the manuscript.

SONGS OF THE WHITE SUN, a collection of 13 favorite folksongs, was first recorded in 1953. It has been preserved in a new, state-of-the-art CD, thanks to Nancy Carruthers Rorty, willing to loan her precious, unscratched copy of the original 12-inch LP recording.

My warm thanks to all!

✖

WHITE SUN

A lone car crosses the open desert on Rio Del Sol (now renamed Bob Hope Drive), which connects Interstate 10 with Highway 111 in Rancho Mirage, California.

February 1955
Helen Dengler Photo

chapter 1
The Awesome Desert

Jack stood grinning in the doorway, hands in his pockets, feet firmly planted in shiny new cowboy boots. His dark eyes sparkled with excitement.

"It's a deal, Helen!"

I wonder are we mad? Investing in a patch of desert sand, located in a place named Rancho Mirage?

"We'll drive down tomorrow," he urged, "and I'll show you The Eleven Mile Ranch. Just wait, Helen. You'll be surprised!"

Tomorrow was St. Patrick's Day, March 17, 1946, my turn to check out Jack's desert property and see what his excitement was all about, turning some derelict old place into a guest ranch!

Bright and early the next morning we loaded Grandma, our woody Dodge station wagon, with supplies and our four children all raring to go, two-year-old Mark, Ian four, and the twins David and Nancy, seven. It was a hundred and twenty-five miles to the desert from our home in Pasadena, California. There were no freeways as yet, and Jack didn't believe in air-conditioned cars. Driving down the long slope from the Banning pass to Palm Springs was like descending into a hot oven.

Jack parked Grandma in front of Tony Burke's Palm Springs real estate office. Tony knew the desert area well and was highly qualified to show Jack all the possibilities.[1] His crisp British speech seemed strangely out of place as he greeted us.

"I've got all the escrow papers ready for you to sign, Jack," he announced.

I signed my name under Jack's, before ever getting a chance to inspect our newly acquired real estate. Two hundred and fifty thousand dollars for ten acres of sand and some weathered old ranch buildings. I thought to myself, this is only the beginning.

Piling back in the sweltering car, questions kept coming. "How much further, Mommy?"

"Now just a minute, fellows. We told you the name of this place is The Eleven Mile Ranch. You tell me how much further?"

The twins guessed, "Eleven Miles?"

"There's a sign, Daddy. Cathedral City. Slow down!"

It would take some stretch of the imagination to call the few buildings we could see, a city, and there was no sign of any cathedral.[2] This "city" looked more like a ghost town to us, no people or cars, just a couple of palm trees. We quickly drove through it and, immediately, were driving again in the hot, open desert.

More miles. Then suddenly living proof before me! U.S. POST OFFICE, RANCHO MIRAGE, CALIFORNIA! Jack had not made it up and it wasn't a mirage! The letters were painted over a small building on our left, looking more like a shack than a post office. Jack slowed down.

"We're almost there."

"Look Mommy there it is, there it is," Nancy shouted, pointing. We all stared at The Eleven Mile Ranch sign.

I was having a sinking feeling. Like other desert structures we had passed, the weather-beaten, hand-lettered sign stood slightly skewed, near a street sign labeled Magnesia Falls Drive.

Where did they get these names? Rancho Mirage? Magnesia Falls Drive?

Bordered by creosote bushes, Magnesia Falls Drive consisted mostly of tumbleweeds and drifting sand invading the roadway all the way down a gentle slope to the ranch entrance. I gasped in amazement at the ranch gate. Pink oleanders in full bloom were flourishing at one side, sprouting from a ditch of flowing water! The marvels of irrigation! Partly screened by a jungle of tamarisk trees further back, I could make out a low building. A

Unpaved Magnesia Falls Drive with the original Eleven Mile Ranch sign. The Shadow Mountains frame the back-drop.

May 1944
A. E. Hainer Photo

water tower with brown shingle siding squatted on its roof, no doubt the source of the irrigation water. One lone fan palm guarded the front door.

Before I could take in any more, a couple suddenly appeared, Colonel A. E. Hainer and his pretty wife. Oh, what charmers! No welcoming committee could have been more cordial or disarming. They had already won over Jack. I was the next target. The Hainers concentrated on putting me at ease, hoping to dispel any negative ideas I might be harboring regarding deserts in general.

Over and over they assured me this particular desert was nothing short of paradise! Paradise indeed for him to breath such pure, dry air! The Colonel had already set about converting the place into a guest ranch, but soon discovered the challenge was too great for his frail health. Turning the place into a guest ranch was a challenge for a younger man. Jack Dengler had materialized at precisely the right moment, a younger man who thrived on challenges.

I began to wilt. The desert heat was getting to me. I glanced longingly at a giant tamarisk tree, its wide branches shading some rustic cabins across the patio. Gray-green needles were raining down from its branches in an almost constant shower, carpeting everything nearby. I would soon discover the desert winds that picked up those tamarisk needles and sand, deposited them in nearly every crevice in the desert.

Colonel Hainer must have read my mind. "Make yourselves right at home, folks," pointing out two of the cabins. "You can't really get any idea of this place without spending a couple of nights." Moving over into the welcome shade, he added, "These cabins formed part of Dr. Earl Tarr's school for asthmatic children, before I bought the place." He offered no further details.

Not until years later, when I became Rancho Mirage Chamber of Commerce secretary, did I manage to unearth more of the ranch's colorful history. I began my research in Riverside, California, checking over documents relating to the Eleven Mile Ranch, which dated back to the days of President Calvin Coolidge (1923–1929). What I found most enlightening, was that Cahuilla Indians[2] had survived in this same desert area and the

4

*Surrounded by a tamarisk jungle,
with an old water tower squatting on
its roof, The Eleven Mile Ranch bears
little resemblance to a future guest
ranch!*

May 1944
Col. A. E. Hainer Photo

5

bordering Santa Rosa Mountains for at least 3,000 years, right up to the present day!

Early twentieth century Rancho Mirage pioneers' survival rate pales in comparison!

The first homesteader to claim the land where we were standing, was William F. Everett, who probably planted the patio's venerable tamarisk tree. In 1925 he staked a claim, calling his homestead "The Eleven Mile Ranch," since it bisected the distance between stagecoach stops in Palm Springs and Indio. During those reckless early twenties, date palm ranchers began developing the Coachella Valley by importing two non-native trees, the date palm and the tamarisk (which served as a windbreak to protect the growing date orchards).

Homesteader Everett chose to plant grapefruit trees. Later on, the date ranchers included grapefruit interplanted with their date palms, since grapefruit produces a faster crop than dates. Everett drilled a well and laid out irrigation lines. He was lucky at first, with adequate water. The southwest was experiencing a wet cycle at that period, and his orchard thrived. But, one winter a severe frost hit, killing all his grapefruit trees except for one lone tree planted at the ranch's kitchen door.

Everett called it quits and sold his ranch to Southland Land and Realty Company. They decided on a different approach, a grandiose scheme to create an Egyptian-style subdivision, a reincarnation of the Nile Valley no less, replete with camels, colorful tents, and why not belly dancers? Speculating on a Hollywood-type extravaganza, rising Phoenix-like from the ashes of Everett's grapefruit ranch, Southland's dream vanished in the Crash of 1929, with the arrival of the Great Depression. There would be no camels, no colorful tents, and no belly dancers.[3]

Harry Jones was the third owner of the Eleven Mile Ranch. He leased the place to Doctor Earl Tarr, a firm believer in the desert's magic healing propensities. During the early thirties in nearby Cathedral City, Dr. Tarr had already established a successful health school for children handicapped by respiratory diseases. But his space was limited. Fortune smiled on Dr. Tarr when his guardian angel, Will Rogers, offered $200,000 dollars to finance moving Tarr's school to The Eleven Mile Ranch and roomier quarters. Tarr renamed the place Hacienda de la Sanidad, where his staff of eight teachers continued to work miracles with asthmatic children.

Then, tragedy.

Will Rogers, the school's chief backer, was killed in an Alaskan air crash, August 15, 1935, along with the pilot, Wiley Post. Hacienda de la Sanidad appeared doomed. But wait! Hollywood to the rescue! A loyal group of Rogers' friends, among them film stars Roz Russell, Mike Romanoff, Basil Rathbone, Mary Pickford, Gary Cooper, Norma Shearer, and Tom Mix, chipped in to keep Tarr's health school afloat for another seven years. When World War II drained away the school's teaching staff in 1941, The Eleven Mile Ranch's third enterprise failed.

A grapefruit ranch, an Egyptian subdivision, a desert health school, all three vanished. Would Colonel Hainer's dream of a guest ranch fare any better? Could a thirty-four-year-old New Yorker, with no hotel experience and no construction background, other than building a few cement block walls in his own backyard, turn The Eleven Mile Ranch into a successful dude ranch?

The Hainers sized me up in a hurry, a suspicious female, with preconceived notions about deserts in general. What else was there to expect from a tenderfoot, freckle-faced redhead, a total novice from the green hills of Wisconsin? To my way of thinking, all deserts should be clearly posted, DANGER! NO TRESPASSING! A desert exemplified the very opposite of every familiar thing I knew and loved.

Yet Jack kept insisting, "You'll like it, Helen," adding with uncanny insight, "You'll learn to love it!"

How could he know? How could our poor children survive in this desert? The whole proposition seemed utterly preposterous.

I should have known better. Since the day we met, Jack had been throwing me challenges, each one seemingly beyond my capabilities.

Asthmatic patients were housed in these rustic cabins when Dr. Earl Tarr took over The Eleven Mile Ranch, renaming it Hacienda de la Sanidad.

May 1944
Col. A. E. Hainer Photo

Time and again he had proven me wrong. I was slow to gain confidence in myself. My instinctive resistance to Jack's ideas merely served to goad him on to greater achievements, a lesson I never quite grasped.

Our first night in the rustic cabins, however, only confirmed my worst suspicions. The floors had no solid base, just slats with large gaps between the boards, where sand poked through. My solution was to tidy up the place, give the floor a good hosing down. The ensuing deluge produced alarming results! An unwelcome visitor with pale claws reached up through the slats. An outraged scorpion! With arched tail at the ready, he aimed his poisonous stinger at me!

To think the Hainers considered this particular desert a paradise? My poor, wee babes sleeping with scorpions? There was more to come. Jack commandeered the twins for a Black Widow Patrol after supper, arming them with brooms to sweep out the poisonous spiders from porches and doorways.

Morning rituals required a careful inspection of clothes and shoes to discover if any desert critters might have moved in during the night. As yet there had been no mention of snakes, but my overwrought imagination pictured the entire desert crawling with rattlesnakes and their smaller cousins, sidewinders. I'd never heard of sidewinders until the day I reached down under some watermelon leaves to turn on a faucet, and discovered the poisonous little snake curled around the handle.

There were more gaps in my education. Those beautiful pink oleanders I had admired at the ranch entrance? They too, were poisonous. The list was becoming overwhelming.

On our second day, as the desert winds grew stronger, strong enough to pit the car's windshield driving down the highway, strong enough to infiltrate closed doors, windows, kitchen cabinets and cupboards, I faced Jack with an ultimatum.

"It's not going to work for me, Jack. You can find someone else to help you build your guest ranch!" I was determined to retreat to a safer, more civilized environment, and to rescue the children from snakes, spiders and scorpions!

Four little Denglers, Ian, Nancy, David and Mark happily cope with dachshund puppies, unaware of a future coping with scorpions and sidewinders.

Pasadena, California
December 3, 1944
Helen Dengler Photo

Driving home to Pasadena from the crystal clear air of the desert, we noticed smog for the first time. Traffic in post-war Los Angeles was creating a brownish pall over the city, and our home in Pasadena was included in that "bowl of soup!" Where to escape?

Since I refused to consider moving to the ranch, we explored other options, finally settling on a house in Montecito, just south of Santa Barbara. There, on the coast a hundred miles northwest of Los Angeles, we felt safely out of the smog belt. I was pregnant with Lori and a lot happier in our comfortable Montecito home.

For the next five years I was a holdout while Jack, without complaint, continued his four-hundred-mile round-trip commute to the desert. After all, he was in the full glory of creation, planning and building his ideal, western dude ranch.

Our first ranch managers, Topsy and Forry Haller find a good way to cool off in the sweltering desert heat.

July 1946
Bruno Photo

chapter 2

Eleven Mile Ranch

Jack wasn't handicapped by my defection. Other workers materialized out of thin air. His creative ferment attracted people like a magnet, just as I had been mesmerized when I met Jack in 1934 on his first European bicycle tour. I started right in working for SITA, his student travel organization.

Topsy and Forry Haller, a young honeymoon couple, were so intrigued with his ideas, they became Jack's first construction crew and ranch managers. Almost half a century later when I wrote to ask them about the ranch, their recollections were still vivid. The Hallers responded with a long letter from Salem, Oregon, June 12, 1992. Topsy explained:

> Forry met Jack when he was working at Northrup Aircraft (during the war), and bumped into him again in Palm Springs, just after Jack bought the Hainers' ranch. We were footloose at the time, and Jack discussed his plans for the creation of what turned out to be the White Sun Guest Ranch. We made a deal to participate in the development of his dream.

> The ranch was quite run-down but still charming, and promising. We moved into the main ranch house and immediately got into cleanup and construction.

Jack found the Hallers eager, courageous, energetic and completely trustworthy. Topsy, besides being gorgeous to look at, proved a talented and resourceful cook. When the curious strayed down Magnesia Falls Drive to see what was a-building on the old Eleven Mile Ranch, they sometimes asked to check in for a few days, a week, maybe longer? The Hallers put them right to work. One of those drifters was Jose. Forry remembered:

> This developed into a very fond relationship, that ended at our parting, with tears in all our eyes. ... Jose knew no English, and Topsy had only high school Spanish. With the help of the dictionary we managed to

communicate and got to know Jose pretty well. He was a tall, dignified man, with a big moustache. Topsy mailed his paycheck to his family in Mexico. One of his sons was going to college. Topsy did all his grocery shopping for him … He worked from sun-up to sun-down, for $5.00 a day.

We started on Jack's mall houses angled out towards the open desert, eight contiguous units all built of cement blocks, and a bunkhouse.

Jack was very impatient, and wanted to see the roof on the bunkhouse, so we put it up before we put in the cross ties. We had the roof pretty well finished, and then happened to look down the long, rear wall. To our horror the wall was sharply tilted out, threatening to collapse! We frantically shored it up and got it back into place, breathing big sighs of relief!

We won't forget the hot summers there. Generally we would get up at daybreak, and work until about ll:00 A.M. Then we would spend about four hours in the house during peak heat periods (around 110 degrees outside), playing pinochle, canasta, or whatever suited our fancy. Then about 3:00 P.M., resume work until dusk … This was hard, heavy work, mixing cement, hauling and laying the concrete blocks.

Mr. Peck, a civil engineer and topnotch mason, intrigued the Hallers. Their letter continues:

He was a unique individual … We learned a great deal about construction, but even more we enjoyed him as a personality … one of the best poker players we have ever encountered. Like so many others, Peck had chosen to live in the desert, due to his bad lungs.

One night the coyotes were howling, as they usually do in the desert, and we became concerned about Diego, the Dengler Dachshund, who was missing. Topsy set out on foot to look for him, in spite of sidewinders and other night creatures. She headed for a spot where there was a particular amount of howling. On her way she ran into Cubbie, our affectionate little dog, dragging Diego back towards the ranch. The coyotes had mauled him severely. We rushed him to the vets, but since there wasn't much they could do, we took him back to the ranch.

Building is Jack's passion. He starts off breaking ground for the bunkhouse. Old barn behind the trees was later moved to the stables area.

April 1946
Forry Haller Photo

15

Forry sketches a Valentine Day's heart in the sand for Topsy.

February 14, 1947
Deane Haller Photo

16

Miraculously, Diego recovered! We felt especially fond of Cubbie, thereafter.

The desert was a pretty lonely place during the summer … Rancho Mirage was just a small village … Palm Desert began after White Sun. With so few people around, we met most of them, including Cliff Henderson, founder of Palm Desert. There were so few accommodations in the area, we had people staying at the ranch, even though it was still in the building process. Topsy did the cooking in very primitive conditions, and we all ate together around the big dining room table in the main room.

Another visitor, Henry (Hank) Gogerty, owner of the little airport adjacent to White Sun, was in the process of setting up Desert Air Park Resort. He had a Waco bi-plane that he flew down to the desert, to visit his resort, his date palm and Thompson seedless grape ranch. We used to play poker and pinochle with him in the evenings.

One night he brought a friend, Glen Odekirk, and subsequently Glen joined our card-playing evenings. We had no idea who these men were, but found out Gogerty was an architect who designed many of the Los Angeles school system buildings, and Odekirk was general manager of the Hughes Aircraft plant in Culver City, and a very close associate of Howard Hughes. This all came out the day after Hughes crashed his experimental fighter. Topsy has a flight log book with two hours of training by Glen, in his Waco. I'll never forget watching her lazily circling above the desert.

Many celebrity types would visit the White Sun, especially during the summer, when not much was going on. Most desert visitors will never forget the desert sandstorms, and we had our share. We actually had to shovel sand out of the buildings, before we could even think of sweeping them, since we hadn't yet enclosed them. This happened many times.

How pleasant it would be during hot weather, to run irrigation ditches to the oleanders, or to use the shallow, old swimming pool that was there on the original place. For air-conditioning we had old-fashioned swamp coolers, that were not very effective. Nor will we forget the frequent encounters with black widow spiders in the old water tower. Forry used to swat them with his hands!

Certainly one of our best recollections is when the Dengler tribe would visit. We thought the world of those kids and enjoyed every visit. Jack was resurrecting his travel business (SITA), after the war ended, so we saw very little of him.

It was fun to know Hedy Lamar had a house close by, and old Frank Morgan had a home up the street, not too far. Looking back it's interesting to think of the city of Palm Springs, center of all desert activity then, and to see the tremendous growth to the south, now …

Another memory of White Sun's early days came from Betty Upton Gates, a member of my 1948 SITA European Bicycle Tour:

The first time I saw it (White Sun), was in late spring 1949. Still in a euphoric state after my 1948 SITA trip, I set off with you to see your new acquisition in property first-hand. We drove the narrow, two-lane highway following the mountains, and much of the road was covered with sand due to a big wind storm the day before.

We had lunch in a small Palm Springs restaurant. From there we proceeded south, and after some time reached the White Sun Guest Ranch. It was deserted, just waiting for you and Jack to work on renovation. Sand was piled up near windows and doors, because of the constant wind … I was awed by the size of the up-coming project, not seeing it through your eyes or Jack's.

Never could I have dreamed that a desert oasis would someday appear, with palm trees, lovely flowers, comfortable rooms, delicious food, horses, breakfast rides, an inviting lounge, dining room, accordion music, funfests galore, and much, much more!

That desert oasis was to become a reality due to entrepreneur Jack, born with the ability to recognize potentialities, and the energy and creativity to make them happen. When World War II exploded, engulfing the world in flames, Jack was forced to invent an alternative to his SITA travel business. He reversed gears. Instead of leading tourists to faraway places, he created one, single, compelling destination for them, in a magical place called Rancho Mirage.

Well before White Sun was fully developed with all its later amenities, people found it a hard place to leave.

Karen Christy wails, "Please Mommy, I don't want to go home!"

November 1964
Helen Dengler Photo

The ranch is shaping up with a red-wood entrance gate and historical marker to welcome guests.

April 1957
Helen Dengler Photo

chapter 3
How Many Bales of Hay?

Jack struck gold when he hired the Hallers as his first ranch managers. They plunged so blithely—and enthusiastically—into the staggering task of ranch renovation and construction. The first phase was off to a good start. Next, the ranch needed a new name. Neither The Eleven Mile Ranch or Hacienda de la Sanidad would do. The name must imply something more descriptive of the desert, compelling, distinctive, a name one could not easily forget.

We circulated a list of suggestions among our friends, eliminating the two most hackneyed words, "palm" and "desert." Jack's combination, WHITE SUN, was the unanimous choice, conjuring up the intensity of the desert sun. Henceforth, WHITE SUN GUEST RANCH it would be.[1] The ranch roads needed names, too: Wagon Wheel Road, Horseshoe Circle, Deglet Drive, Eleven-Mile Road, and SITA PLATZ, named when Jack moved his travel headquarters from New York City to Rancho Mirage.

In 1947, when Topsy and Forry left the desert, a search for new managers began in earnest. Optimist Jack had figured the ranch would generate enough income to finance his post-war recovery of SITA Travel. It didn't take him long to discover SITA had to finance the development of the ranch! Any surplus was immediately plowed back into new units, a well, sport facilities, a list without end. White Sun always seemed in need of more funds.

For our second managers, we found a couple willing to invest some of their savings in the ranch, but that fortunate arrangement lasted only one season. Back to the search again.

A third and more flamboyant chapter opened in 1948, with the arrival of an intriguing couple who might well have walked right off a Hollywood movie set. Being dude ranch novices, Jack and I were much impressed by

21

our first interview with this striking pair. They were eager and they were available. We hired them immediately. A cowboy stereotype, lean and handsome, deeply tanned, dashing hat, boots and buckles, our new manager towered over Jack's five foot seven inches. His statuesque wife was an opera singer, a star, with a velvety soprano and an extraordinary vocal range.

For almost two years, they kept us successfully hoodwinked, while exploiting White Sun as their own exclusive ranch, enjoying nude swimming parties in the pool, with a shotgun handy to scare off any peeping Toms. When we finally discovered too many bookkeeping discrepancies, their party was over. They left us two legacies, our monumental redwood entrance gate, and a haunting theme song, WHITE SUN AND PURPLE SAGE, composed by the diva herself.

Enter Virginia Kraft, and her husband, Phil, White Sun's fourth set of managers. Virginia was competent, down to earth, and gracious. She saw to it that guests were comfortable and at home. Phil, quiet and efficient, looked after the grounds. With a solid reputation as managers, they restored the friendly ambience at White Sun that Jack had first imagined, attracting new guests, who returned again and again. They made contact with artists and musicians, and were responsible for bringing down the San Francisco opera crowd. When San Francisco Opera Director, Kurt Herbert Adler arrived with his elegant wife Diantha, the chemistry was unforgettable. Memorable and happy musical years were to follow!

But Jack wanted me at the ranch. During those five early years of adjustment and turmoil, my resistance to moving from Santa Barbara to the desert was weakening. We had already set up a SITA office in our Santa Barbara home in 1947, where I spent many a sleepless night with a dictaphone, struggling to keep abreast of the post-war travel boom. SITA was offering more tours to more destinations around the world, to cope with this phenomenal growth. Our family, too, had expanded from four to five, with the arrival of Lori in 1947.

My Aunt Helen K. Dunning, Mother's sister, who had helped her raise the five of us Dykemas, came to my rescue in 1943, agreeing to live with us when Mark was born. She was a most welcome member of our family. Trained as a baby nurse and a marvelous cook, Aunt Helen dearly loved

Fleeing to Switzerland after escaping the Nazis, Paulus Geheeb and his wife Edith, founders of the Odenwaldschule near Heidelberg, Germany, relocated their international, coeducational boarding school in the Bernese Alps. They renamed it Ecole d'Humanité. At different times from 1948 to1951, four Dengler children attended the Ecole.

Goldern, Switzerland 1948
H. Cassirer Photo, Verlag R. Würgler, Meiringen, Switzerland

the children. She made it possible for me to conduct my ninth bicycle tour, when war-torn Europe welcomed back tourists in 1948, but made one important stipulation after Lori was born. With both parents on tour, three of the five Dengler children would be enough for her to handle!

So I took Nancy and Ian along with me to Europe for the summer of 1948, enrolling them at the Ecole d'Humanité in Switzerland's Bernese Alps. David and Mark attended the Ecole the next summer, and David returned for a full school year in 1951–52.

Paulus and Edith Geheeb, co-founders and directors of the Odenwaldschule near Heidelberg, Germany (where in 1931 I had been privileged to receive the most enlightening educational experience of my life), had fled Nazi Germany to seek refuge in Switzerland. After desperate struggles during the war, Paulus established a new Swiss school in Goldern, renaming it Ecole d'Humanité. This remarkable international, coeducational boarding school still flourishes in the 21st Century, attracting students from all over the world.

In 1948, when European travel was once more authorized after the war, Jack was off and running, opening a network of SITA offices around the world. There was little time for the ranch or his family. Yet on all those flying trips, besides his SITA work load, he never ceased dreaming up improvements for White Sun. Most of all he wanted his family firmly in charge of the ranch, where he was planning, eventually, to move SITA headquarters.

In the fall of 1951, I finally gave in, agreeing to abandon Santa Barbara and become manager of White Sun. For the next twenty-three years, we all were rooted in the desert!

I began this new life with considerable trepidation. My hotel experience was limited to being a guest, never a manager. And a guest ranch is much more than a hotel. I had a great deal to learn, including coming to terms with horses!

Palm Springs celebrated the opening of the desert's fall season with a Western Week Parade down Palm Canyon Drive, the city's main thoroughfare. As a guest ranch manager, I was invited to join the parade on horseback, carrying the essential props, an American flag in one hand, and a bottle of beer in the other. Refusing the invitation was out of the question.

What about the horse's reins? In the first place, unencumbered with props, I didn't know how to ride. But I could learn, so I agreed to ride in the parade.

Western clothes were mandatory and, as yet, completely lacking in my wardrobe. Off I went to Palm Springs, to buy the correct outfit, which included skin-tight, pin-striped wool trousers, western shirt, bolo tie, cowboy boots, silver buckles, turquoise collar tips and rings, plus a dashing cowboy hat.

So far so good. Next, a horse, please!

Our assistant wrangler, Johnson, assured me he had the perfect, gentle mount for a beginner, "Black Hawk," a handsome gelding. "Piece of cake, Helen," he assured me. "You'll be ridin' in no time!" Western Week loomed a short two weeks away. In no time at all I was to jump into Black Hawk's, as well as White Sun's managerial saddle!

Black Hawk was undeniably handsome, but not as gentle and amiable as Johnson had predicted. In order to climb into his saddle I quickly learned to put my foot in the stirrup facing backwards, since he would immediately charge forwards, flinging me willy-nilly onto his back.

Johnson's lessons paid off. I was catching on, seeing the desert from a new perspective, high on Black Hawk's back. It was intoxicating! He was a dancer/prancer, who dearly loved galloping full speed down the desert washes. If I had to fall, there was only sand below, and I wasn't worried. For the parade, I decided to hang on to the reins with one hand, and pass on the bottle of beer!

Parade Day arrived in blinding sunshine, a scorching 100 degrees. First came the parade line-up, an interminable hour of jockeying about. Black Hawk pranced excitedly up and down, making cheese-graters of my scratchy, new wool pants. Once we moved out along Palm Canyon Drive, I was convinced Black Hawk and I would crash through I. Magnin's display windows. It was all I could do to stay in the saddle.

Somehow I managed to hang on until the bitter end, vowing this would be my first and last parade!

Jumping into the ranch manager's saddle was a much bigger challenge than Black Hawk's, but I was lucky. I inherited a supportive staff, a large plus. First in order of importance, there was Hazel the chef, heart and soul of the operation. If the cook is no good, everything falls apart. Hazel was an artist who wrought magic in her kitchen. She set the mood for the entire day, for all the staff ate together in the kitchen, before guests were served. Nothing but the best! Keep everybody happy!

We lucked out again for office workers, kitchen help, waiters, maintenance crews and maids. Jack hand-picked and trained all SITA leaders for the summer tours, so why not bring the best of them over from Europe, to work the winter shift at the ranch? With few exceptions, on-the-job training was the hallmark of White Sun's staff. Though we required well-trained professionals as chef, wrangler, and bookkeeper, the rest of the staff tackled assignments with enthusiasm, but little or no real hotel experience. Hiring young SITA tour leaders already trained in public relations, as well as SITA alumni, proved to be remarkably effective and profitable for us all.

Marianne Bohn, from Aachen, Germany, and Birthe Andersen from Copenhagen, Denmark, were both ready to come. As tour leaders they had plenty of experience handling people, and their fresh young faces and fetching foreign accents were a big hit with ranch guests. Jack felt these European girls needed some orientation en route from Europe to California, so he provided them with steamer tickets to Montreal, and cross-country Greyhound Bus tickets via the southern states to California.

The girls knew there would be few opportunities to get any sleep so they chose the back seat of the bus, where they could stretch out. In 1952, the back of the bus was reserved for blacks in the southern states, much to the girls' bewilderment. When they courteously greeted blacks or whites anywhere, or stumbled into segregated restrooms or restaurants, "What country are you from?" became a frequent question.

In Tennessee, when they greeted a tall gentleman with a cheery "Good Morning," he asked, "Where are you going?" When they told him California,

SITA tour leaders, Marianne Bohn from Germany, and Birthe Andersen from Denmark, move into temporary trailer quarters, to join the White Sun staff.

Fall 1953
Helen Dengler Photo

It's not all work and no play for "Les Girls," ranch staffers Marianne, Birthe, Helen and Nancy Carruthers.

Easter 1954
Jan Rouse Photo

he offered them a stack of American comic books, adding, "That will keep you busy!" Marianne and Birthe didn't know what comic books were, but thanked him, and gladly accepted them.

Racial bias was not just a peculiarity of the South, the girls discovered. One hot day when Marianne was working in the ranch kitchen, a black delivery boy came to the back door with a large package. She offered to help him bring it in, which he would not hear of, and then she offered him a glass of cold orange juice.

"Can I ask you a personal question? We are not used to being treated like that."

"Like what?" Marianne responded, so he asked,

"What country are you from?"

Many years later when I asked Marianne how often she heard that question, she laughed. "Oh, many times and I made wonderful friends."

Working at Jack's guest ranch also sounded like a great idea to some of those SITA travelers, footloose and fancy free after their tours. That included Bill Cunningham and Kathy Maclean who took turns spelling me in the office. Jan Rouse, became our public relations director for both SITA on the West Coast, and White Sun. And I'm sure Nancy Carruthers was born riding a horse. She was not only a competent wrangler, she also played the accordion!

So how was I faring in my new role as manager?

It didn't take long for wholesalers to figure out White Sun had a novice manager, a good place for a sale. Since I had no idea how many cans of tomato soup to order, or pounds of New York steak, or rolls of toilet paper, I'd cautiously buy a few items from each salesman who showed up at the back door and sort them out later.

Another large blank in my education was the stables. Our wrangler Al asked me how many bales of hay to order. Logically that seemed a matter

Boss of the stables, wrangler Al Hein.

March 1957
Helen Dengler Photo

"Great job Bill!" SITAGRAM editor
Helen compliments the print shop
boss, Bill Kephart on a SITAGRAM
newsletter hot off the press.

September 1953
Paul Pospesil Photo

for him to decide. Curious thing about horse people. They don't reason the way most people do. Why should wrangler Al Hein ask me how many bales of hay to order? That made no sense. Al was a splendid wrangler, knew his job, kept his riders safe and happy, and coming back for more. I was not a horse person. I had no idea how many bales of hay a horse could eat!

Bookkeeper Lee Pagliotti, an acquaintance from Santa Barbara, shared my cubbyhole office. Tall, dark and exotic, with penetrating black eyes, Lee enjoyed fortune telling with tarot cards, and was often sought out by curious guests in the lobby after dinner. During one memorable séance with a guest, she predicted dire consequences regarding extra-marital affairs. This precipitated a hasty check out and that gentleman's speedy return home to his wife!

I stayed clear of Hazel's kitchen. That was her territory and make no mistake! My responsibilities were the front office; keeping guests occupied and happy, depending on their interests and ambitions; playing my accordion in the bar; joining in a round of Scrabble or THE Game; or arranging outings. Perhaps a day trip to Joshua Tree National Monument (now a National Park), the Mecca Hills, or Idyllwild, high above us in the snow. Maybe they'd enjoy a day of water-skiing at the Salton Sea, or a hike up Magnesia Falls Canyon.

Aside from family responsibilities, I was also SITA's public relations director, writing the SITAGRAM and the ranch newsletter WHITE SUN ROUND-UP which kept guests informed of ranch doings, people, and exciting new developments.

Discovering the bucolic delights of Clancy Lane, only a few minutes ride from the ranch, was an exciting new adventure for me. The lane was named after L. M. and Helen Clancy, escapees from Los Angeles who both longed for a simpler lifestyle. In 1932 they pioneered their desert ranch without the comforts of electricity, telephone or air conditioning. They hand-made the adobe bricks to build their house, and planted grapefruit trees, date palms, and a vineyard. They loved animals. When they eventually gave into the luxuries of electric lights and running water, they even invited their pet goats in to their home to watch television!

I was so taken with "Sissy," one of their goats, the Clancys let me borrow her for the 1962 Brazilian Carnival we staged at White Sun. Any good carnival includes an impromptu wedding, so we had to arrange one also. John Kennedy played the part of the padre, officiating in Portuguese, while Sissy the goat stood docilely by his side. The pregnant bride (Helen) and her groom (Jack) decided it was about time to tie the knot, after six children …

Mr. Clancy was very fond of his geese. He had trained his large flock to fly at his command, taking off from the ground like a flight of bombers!

Further down Clancy Lane lived the biologist Lloyd Tevis, his attractive wife Nona, and their two daughters. Their secluded home with a picturesque lily pond was sheltered beneath stately Washingtonia fan palms. Lloyd was soon to play an important role in my continuing desert education.

I was learning so many new things, I had no time to worry about scorpions or sidewinders anymore!

A neighbor, L. M. Clancy, shows me the flock of pet geese he trained on his Clancy Lane ranch, just off Rio Del Sol.

March 1963
Helen Dengler Photo

At White Sun's first SITA Reunion alumni Mickey Kerr, Mary Polk, Barry Wetherby and Joanne Whittier cycle out to explore the desert. Nancy May de l'Arbre sees them off at the gate.

January 5, 1952
Jan Rouse Photo

34

chapter 4

SITA Reunions

1956 . . . . . Japan	1963 . . . . . China
1958 . . . . . Africa	1964 . . . . . Viking
1959 . . . . . Greece	1965 . . . . . Philippines
1960 . . . . . India	1966 . . . . . Ireland
1961 . . . . . Tahiti	1967 . . . . . Iran (Persia)
1962 . . . . . Brazil & Germany	1968 . . . . . Thailand

White Sun was a made-to-order stage for SITA reunions. Former SITA tour members being our most valuable resource, we kept in touch through a SITAGRAM newsletter and annual reunions. SITA, short for Students' International Travel Association, was Jack's 1933 brainstorm while a student in Munich, Germany, exploring the countryside with fellow students on bicycles.[1] What better way is there for young people to learn about the world and each other he decided, than from the seat of a bicycle?

Back in New York City that following winter, Jack worked out a plan of action. He started by organizing and conducting a group of American students to Germany, Austria, Belgium and France. He named his group simply, STUDENT BICYCLE TOUR OF EUROPE, and listed it at the all-inclusive Depression cost of $290.00, for a ten-week summer, including round-trip Third Class steamer transportation!

At the stroke of midnight on June 27, 1934, twenty-two-year-old entrepreneur Jack Dengler, with his small group of nine boys, embarked on the S. S. ALBERT BALLIN, of the Hamburg-American Line, on what would become the most far-reaching, successful business adventure of his life.

"Cheap Jitney service to all points." Conductor Frank Dupuy's 1914
Metropolitan Rapid Transit Co. Jitney Bus makes the 120-miles from
San Gabriel to the ranch in seven hours. More members of Helen's
1953 E-1J European cycle tour are packed in the jitney bus.

January 9, 1954
Photos courtesy Frank Dupuy

It so happened my brother, Peter Scot Dykema and I also embarked on that same steamer. We went our separate ways after arriving in Europe, but a month later decided to meet Jack in Munich. He persuaded us to join his cyclists for twelve eventful days in the Bavarian Alps that changed my life forever.

The following summer after my junior year at Barnard College, I joined the SITA European bandwagon as Jack's assistant tour leader. Back home in New York City three months later, I made up my mind. A formal wedding played no part in my decision to elope with Jack on my 21st birthday, a marriage that lasted sixty-three years until Jack's death in 1998.

SITA groups tripled each summer, mushrooming after the war into a worldwide tour wholesaler, SITA WORLD TRAVEL INC., with offices around the globe. Jack logged countless hours and air miles, personally investigating and opening up new destinations, developing tours that went in all directions, designed for both domestic and foreign travelers.

During those long hours of global air travel, carrying a small Olivetti typewriter to write his SITA reports, a light raincoat, and not much else, Jack never ceased dreaming up improvements for the ranch. These he implemented during his brief touchdowns in the desert. White Sun flourished, expanding like SITA, but not on so grand a scale.

Before World War II SITA tours took a leisurely approach to Europe by steamer, with plenty of time to adjust to entirely different cultures. From that very first day of the Atlantic steamer crossing, tour members began developing strong ties, through well-organized daily language lessons, history, art, music, and deck setting-up exercises in preparation for cycling.

An Italian SITA leader once told me, "I know each tour member better than I know the members of my own family!" That was no surprise. SITA groups lived together twenty-four hours a day for two or three months, housed in youth hostel dormitories and small inns.

Before White Sun came into the picture, SITA reunions were pretty casual affairs. Following the war the public's pent-up longing to travel caused a veritable explosion in tourism. This caused a corresponding increase in the number and variety of SITA tours, swelling the numbers of SITA alumni.

Gathered in the patio for sunshine and songs, early SITA reunions were casual affairs with no specific theme. Starting in 1956, a different foreign country was honored every year.

January 6, 1952
Lee Wenzlick Photo

Guest of honor Eleanor Roosevelt, in her address at the New York SITA reunion, stressed the value of student travel and the need to "really see a country." She is surrounded by Columbia University's Professor Frederic Hoffherr, a member of SITA's Board of Directors, Wiley Pickett, New York SITA Manager, John Duprios and President Jack Dengler.

Hotel Shelton ballroom, New York City
December 29, 1953
Nelly's Photo

There were more and more reunions taking place around the country, but the prize party of all took place at White Sun, heart and nerve center of SITA's vast travel organization.

In a move unprecedented in the travel industry, Jack shifted his SITA Headquarters in 1958 from New York City's Fifth Avenue to his ranch in the California desert. This effectively consolidated SITA operations with White Sun. "The jet age has made the desert as likely a place as any city location, for our headquarters. ... In many ways our new location offers advantages, such as space for expansion, and staff amenities, which no city can provide."

What he didn't mention, the move meant less separation from his family and the ranch. Hidden away behind grapefruit trees, the SITA Wing, and Print Shop, caused no interference with the guest ranch operation, but actually enhanced it.

To present reunions as a celebration of White Sun's fall opening for the Palm Springs winter season soon became an annual tradition. Each reunion honored a different foreign country. To recreate a theme country's festival as authentically as possible, research and careful planning began at least a year in advance.

White Sun's chef, Jean Schaffer played a vital role in the success of these reunions. No matter what outrageous menus were required, Jean remained unflappable, rising to the challenge as each foreign invasion swept over her premises.

It was a stroke of good fortune when Jack found Mitch and Jean Schaffer, a couple from Pennsylvania who could perform dual roles. When the ranch closed in the intense heat of the desert summer, the Schaffers conducted SITA's teenage Western U.S. tours. During the winters, Mitch became White Sun groundskeeper, and chef Jean ruled the kitchen.

For the Greek Reunion she served delectable Moussaka; Adobong Manok At Baboy for the Philippines; Sabzi for Persia; Kaeng Masaman Kai Rue Neua for Thailand. Directions for Tahitian Puaa Himaa, suckling pig, called for roasting in an underground pit, but that didn't faze Jean in the least.

Gemuetlichkeit reigns at the festive outdoor Oktoberfest reunion.

October 13, 1962
Paul Pospesil Photo

43

Christel Maas, AFS exchange student from Bremen, Germany, sings for the Oktoberfest with Lori and sock-betasseled Linda Jones, Emery Slocum and Lissa.

October 13, 1962
Paul Pospesil Photo

A Bavarian Oktoberfest was chosen for SITA's 30th Annual Reunion in 1962, honoring the country where SITA was conceived, as well as Jack's German heritage. At age sixteen, his father John C. Dengler, Sr. emigrated from Bruchsal, Germany, to the States, and his mother, Emma Hirsch Dengler was born of German parents in New York City.

Gemuetlichkeit, a word for which there is no English equivalent, became the order of the day for the Oktoberfest. Roughly translated Gemuetlichkeit means an exuberant outpouring of joyful living, symbolized by togetherness, humor and good fellowship.

Oktoberfest origins go back to the wedding of King Ludwig the First, on October 17, 1810, as part of his wedding entertainment. The meadow where the wedding took place was named Theresien Wiese, after Ludwig's bride, Theresa. White Sun's out-door Oktoberfest took place under a starry desert sky, on the ranch's newly created "Theresien Terrasse."

A San Francisco bakery supplied us with huge, edible Oktoberfest pretzels. We mounted them on Bavarian maypoles, crowned with greenery and festive ribbons to line our Theresien Terrasse. Loewenbrau draft beer flowed into steins from Munich's world-famous Hofbrauhaus. In Los Angeles, we discovered a Schuhplattler Bavarian Band for the polka contest, and a sausage kitchen for the prerequisite Weisswurst.

Carol Collins, SITA's Detroit representative created an enchanting, life-size "Muenchner Kindl" doll made out of papier-mâché, the Oktoberfest poster symbol. In case any other props or reunion supplies were missing, we could always call on SITA offices or alumni located around the country and abroad, to come to our rescue.

China became the reunion focus in 1963. For the Chinese Lantern Festival Charlie Kwok, SITA's resourceful Hong Kong manager shipped us three huge crates of delicate, colorful lanterns made of bamboo frames, paper and silk. They came in wondrous shapes. There were butterflies, dragons, fishes, double coins, peaches, prawns, round walking horses, phoenixes, as well as conventional fringed and tasseled lanterns.The prize crate held a ferocious, dragon-like paper lion's head to lead the costume parade.

*Mandarin Jack introduces his family
at the Chinese Reunion: Lissa, Ian,
Al Goldschmidt, Lori, Mark, Helen
and Nancy.*

October 5, 1963
Palm Springs LIFE Photo

Mounted on the diving board, a Viking longboat ready for launching, is the creation of shipbuilder Mark, who plays the heroic Ragnar the Red at the SITA Viking Reunion.

October 8, 1964
Helen Dengler Photo

Ready to announce the Viking Reunion with a fanfare on an authentic, ancient Lur, Ragnar the Red (Mark) stands with Princess Thora (Lori) beside his Viking longboat.

October 17, 1964
Paul Pospesil Photo

48

Handsome calligraphy banners quoting Chinese philosophers, waved from long poles surrounding "White Sun Moon's" dining area. Charlie Kwok's sister Lillian, the calligraphy artist, began as a SITA trainee and became a permanent staff member at the ranch. From Robert Chu's SITA Taipei office, a Taiwanese two-seater pedicab arrived. Pedicab driver Mark Dengler ferried SITA ladies, dressed to the nines in Mandarin elegance, through a moon-gate to the gold and crimson stage pagoda.

The Lantern Festival brought tears of joy and homesickness to the three Chinese performers, the musicians Luis Tsun-Yuen, Pipa player extraordinaire and Butterfly Harp artist and folksinger, Celia Chung. Frank Que, female impersonator, enthralled the crowd performing the Lantern Dance.

On her 1959 honeymoon trip to Russia and Scandinavia, Nancy attended the Danish Viking Festival in Frederikssund, making her the obvious choice to be coordinator of SITA's 1964 Viking Reunion. Not only did she plan the event, the program and menu, draw the program cover, she wrote the script, sewed the costumes, produced, performed in, and directed THE SAGA OF RAGNAR LODBROK—THE DANE KING, her play about the real-life, 10th Century hero. Nancy always had a flair for drama! This ambitious project was staged at "Whitesunhalla" starring most of the Dengler family, SITA and ranch staff, and recruited volunteers. Lissa and Lori played the princesses Aslog and Thora. Nancy was Hela, Queen of the Underworld. Even Jack participated as King Ella of Northumbria, wearing a long white beard and crown, with Helen as his Viking Queen! White Sun guests were encouraged to participate in the merriment, whether or not they had ever heard of SITA. Invited dignitaries, the Royal Consuls of Denmark, Norway and Sweden, and the Honorary Consul of Finland played the roles of "Royal Chiefs from Foreign Lands." At White Sun the name of the game was participation.

With a large sprinkling of ingenuity and last-minute innovation the final reunion productions brought out hidden talent reminiscent of the real-life crises we had overcome during the course of actual SITA tours. Chef Jean's challenge was to find an outdoor spit large enough to roast an entire ox. It was later devoured by all the Vikings present in the 10th century manner, without benefit of silverware!

To illuminate this drama with 10th century lighting, Mitch Schaffer came up with an ingenious solution, flaming torches made from tin cans filled with gasoline-soaked rolls of toilet paper, mounted on tall standards.

Guests arriving before the big Festival Day watched Mark Dengler create a mighty Viking long-ship on the diving board, ready for launch in "Whitesunfjord" (the swimming pool). He equipped this masterpiece with warriors' shields clamped to its sides, a blazing red and white striped sail, and a fierce dragon-headed prow. (After the reunion, Mark donated the dragon head to the Scandinavian Travel Commission.) At twilight, Mark transformed himself into Ragnar Lodbrok, son of King Sigurd Ring of Sweden, acting the hero's role in Nancy's play. He was resplendent in boots, cloak, a helmet with curved horns, and a chain mail vest of armor he'd made himself in a welding class at college!

Elsie Redman Nelson, a SITA tour veteran, asked "Why is SITA's White Sun Guest Ranch like a chameleon? Because it transforms itself at will! Once a year it becomes a South Sea Island, Munich's Theresien Terrasse, a Viking stronghold, a Philippine Village, or a Medieval Castle in Ireland!"

A medieval castle in the middle of the California desert? Lo and behold a crenelated White Sun tower ablaze with heraldic banners. Standing at the ramparts, trumpeters blew fanfares to announce SITA's 1966 Irish Medieval Banquet for the lords and ladies, singers, dancers, court jesters and leprechauns gathering in the courtyard below.

Ian Dengler, the architect of SITA's Irish Reunion, was inspired by an irresistible personal invitation from Bord Failte, the Irish Tourist Board, addressed to Jack, Helen and Ian, for a chauffeured tour of Ireland, during the merry, merry month of May 1965, the peak month of Irish spring. We were greeted on our arrival by whole mountainsides glowing pink with blooming rhododendrons.

For me, the highlights of that unforgettable Irish journey included a visit to Navan, County Meath, north of Dublin, my Irish grandmother Katie Cargan's birthplace, and Bunratty Castle in the south, not far from Shannon's International Airport.

Bunratty Castle Singers thrill the crowd at the Irish Medieval Banquet: Cora Ryan, Una Kelly, Mary McElliott, Olive Bowyer, Breda Donovan and harpists Fionuala O'Sullivan and Mary McEvoy.

October 15, 1966
Paul Pospesil Photo

51

Bunratty Castle stages a traditional 15th century Medieval Banquet nightly, with magnificent pageantry and the glorious Bunratty Singers. We were so taken by the perfection of their blended voices, elegant costumes and charming faces, we began planning for an Irish SITA Reunion the next year. And wouldn't it be grand to have the Bunratty Singers come too! Fate was more than kind. In the fall of 1966 the Irish Tourist Board sent the Bunratty Singers on a promotional tour of the U.S. West Coast and Canada, and booked them to appear at our White Sun Irish Reunion!

Bunratty Castle was built in the 15th century by the McNamaras on the site of earlier castles. Ireland is riddled with no less than 22,000 castles in various stages of decay, but some have been restored like Bunratty. It became the seat of the O'Brien Kings of Thomond and was besieged by the Confederates in 1647. Admiral William Penn was in command of the defenders and his son William, founder of Pennsylvania, was in the castle during the siege.

Those seven, talented Bunratty Singers must go down in White Sun history. Fionuala O'Sullivan and Mary McEvoy brought along their Irish harps. The others included Mary McElligott, Una Kelly, Olive Bowyer, Breda O'Donovan and Cora Ryan. And I must not fail to mention two little girls, Catriona Bradley and Eileen Malone, who demonstrated Irish jigs and reels so energetically, never moving their upper bodies!

Costumed guests were announced as Lord O'This and Lady McThat as they entered White Sun's Great Hall. The Lord and Lady of the Castle, Jack and Helen greeted their guests with the "Bread of Friendship," dipped in salt, and a hot posset cup of milk curdled with spiced wine.

"Slainte 'gus Saol agat!" "Health and long life to you!"

Guests began drifting off to their rooms after all the festivities had come to an end, the enchanting music, the jigs and reels, the buffoonery of the jesters. However Bunratty Singers and various Irish dignitaries were not ready to call it a day. Inside they gathered around the ranch piano, to sing more nostalgic Irish songs.

Jack presents dancers Ana and Ora Prachasaisoradej at the Loy Krathong Thailand Festival Reunion.

October 23, 1968
Paul Pospesil Photo

We celebrated Loy Krathong to honor Thailand in 1968. People from all walks of life annually gather for this Thai festival of thanksgiving for life-giving waters and a purging of all sins and calamities. Thousands of little boats glittering with tiny, flickering candles are launched on water surfaces throughout the kingdom.

Reunion veteran, Elsie Redman Nelson, reported on the Loy Krathong SITA Thai Festival:

"We all knew this year's theme was Thailand, and we met in the ranch recreation room after lunch to work on 'Krathongs,' miniature boats fashioned of banana leaves filled with flowers, incense, coins and betel nuts. White Sun supplied us with Styrofoam for the boats, quantities of wax flowers and incense candles."

Elsie's report described the elaborate feast, the shadow puppet films and the bewitching Thai dancers. "To climax the entire evening, each guest stepped forward to launch his little flower boat on the quiet waters of the ranch 'Klong' [pool], accompanied by the deep reverberations of a gong. Light points from each floating candle slowly spread over the entire surface of the water."

Symbolic in more ways than one, the Thai Reunion brought down a final curtain on Jack's unique, 36-year-old travel business. Since he believed the golden years of travel were past, he sold SITA to Diners Club in 1969. Then he converted the empty SITA ranch headquarters into guest units as he had done twice before, providing room for more guests.

A giant tamarisk shades the patio where Lynn Morgan is about to ring the dinner bell. Make way for a mad scramble!

1962
Helen Dengler Photo

chapter 5

The Ever Changing Oasis

And somehow on the white-washed walls,
The well-kept flag-stoned walks, the hearthside browns,
The somber colors of the hills that frown,
Diaphanous magentas I'd lay over,
Here at White Sun.

For colors are not "colors in a tube,"
Oh no! They need to breathe and come alive.
They need to feed the heart so they too thrive
From life itself, as well they seem to do,
Here at White Sun.

—Milton Heimlich,[1] 1959

Driving through the massive redwood gateway to White Sun, one entered a secret garden, heady with the scent of petunias massed around an emerald circle of lawn. On one side of the curving driveway, oleanders laden with white blossoms bowed to the ground. On the other, majestic date palms reached for the sky, sheltering citrus lit up like Christmas trees, with golden globes of grapefruit. The White Sun insignia blazed high on the ranch tower, mirrored even higher on the blades of a windmill, which became a desert landmark.

The breezeway entrance drew you in to a wide flagstone patio circling a fountain, towards a giant tamarisk tree,[2] which shaded cabins and a bunkhouse on the left. Across the patio on the right stood the original ranch building, renovated and enlarged to accommodate a western lobby, game room, dining area, kitchen and the Round-Up Room bar.

More enticements lay beyond: a shuffleboard court, and a badminton court that also served for volley ball and outdoor square dances. Still further out, the first swimming pool, sun worshippers' headquarters. Guest units fanned out in a wide V on either side, to reveal the open desert, pristine, uncluttered, a limitless sea of sand. Chance rains could transform that sand into a limitless sea of purple sand verbena and white evening primrose. A graceful, curving retaining wall neatly separated the patio, guest units and pool from the desert. Off to the south a pitch and putt golf course framed the distant Shadow Mountains.

White Sun's first builders, Jack and Forry Haller were amateur architects. But Jack considered himself, "… a pretty good brick layer, fair plumber, and a reasonably good electrician," after his initial trials and errors. Forry was already a competent wood worker.

As for that "fair plumber," Jack's enthusiasm came on a little too strong, when he asked me to check out the toilet in the bunkhouse, before the bathroom even had walls! "Go ahead and try it, Helen. It flushes!"

That's the way the ranch grew, like Topsy. Ideas spun off the top of Jack's head. He had spent summers with SITA groups at various dude ranches in Montana and Wyoming, and he knew what he wanted.

Repairs and additions on the old ranch building were already too far along before we realized tearing down the place and starting from scratch would have been a sounder plan financially. In time it proved a wiser plan to retain the aura of The Eleven Mile Ranch's venerable past. Jack kept this in mind. His added changes and improvements assured White Sun guests the ranch would remain a welcoming, friendly oasis. Informality was the rule, where people, from day one, would always be on a first-name basis.

Much as he reveled being in the midst of the building process, the post-war travel boom demanded Jack's presence at the SITA New York Headquarters, and abroad, allowing him only sporadic visits to the ranch. It was time to turn the building project over to Jim Ramsay. Amiable, versatile Jim became Chief of Ranch Construction in 1948. He was the descendant of a long line of builders from Peebles, Scotland. Jim could tackle anything, including a little gelding job Jack sent home from Tahiti.

"I'm gonna grab that wheelbarrow," says Lynn Morgan. *"Oh no you don't,"* counters Jim Ramsay, ranch construction chief with his able assistant Dick Krings.

July 1960
Helen Dengler Photo

59

Jack, center, takes time out for volley ball on the badminton court. The bunkhouse, one of his building efforts, hides behind an oleander hedge in the background.

1955
Lee Wenzlick Photo

Jack had fallen under the spell of Polynesian Tikis on his visits to Tahiti. Tikis are idols, carved in stone or wood. Throughout Polynesia the wise and potent ancestor Tiki was recognized as the creator of the human race. Carvings show Tiki as a squat, heavy figure of inscrutable mien and menacing power, hands clasped over a protruding belly, large, round eyes, a flat but prominent nose, and an elliptical mouth. Great emphasis was placed on his sexual powers. Orgies were held to stimulate Tiki's sexuality and thereby increase the fertility of the land.

Tikis come in many sizes, miniatures you can hold in your hand, to life-size giants. Jack chose life-size giants, carved in wood. They would do nicely for guardians at White Sun's entrance. He ordered a pair crated and shipped off to the ranch.

When our 1960 manager, Si Slocum, unpacked the Tikis' crate, revealing them in all their naked glory, he was less than amused. Time for a conference with Jim Ramsay. Ramsay called in his assistant, Dick Krings. With ear-to-ear grins, Dick took over the gelding. The cherished Polynesian symbol of fertility yielded to Dick's saw job!

Tikis were just some of the treasures Jack shipped home to the ranch. During another South Seas trip he described an evening in a New Zealand nightclub.

> I suddenly looked up and right in front of me was a large painting of a tuba player ... a rather grotesque character, blowing his tuba with such love and affection, I became enamored. Then I noticed a whole collection of similar paintings around the room ... all painted with a kind of happiness.

On impulse Jack phoned the artist David Kennedy, who said yes, his paintings were for sale. Jack bought the lot. A part-time cartoonist, Kennedy had an intriguing penchant for band musicians. He painted the reflections of scenes inside the shiny bells of the musicians' horns. White Sun's walls soon displayed Kennedy's art.

In the ranch Round-Up Bar, Fijian tapa cloths adorned the walls, along with dozens of foreign currency bills. But we had to draw the line when our New Delhi SITA office manager, Inder Sharma, wanted to send White

The Dengler children's second floor apartment overlooked a pool and the badminton and shuffleboard game area. The stairway approach led up to a large sundeck.

November 1955
Helen Dengler Photo

62

Sun a baby elephant from India!

When Jack finally succeeded in moving the Dengler family in 1951 from Santa Barbara to the ranch, there was no place to house the children. That year thirteen-year-old David was studying at a Swiss school, the Ecole d'Humanité. At the ranch, his twin, Nancy, brothers Ian and Mark, all slept in an old, nine-foot trailer. Four-year-old Lori shared our bedroom. This was strictly a temporary arrangement until Jack completed a new children's wing the following year.

Down came the old metal garage by the kitchen, and in its place Ramsay built a large, two-story unit. The ground floor included three guest rooms, a big recreation room, a kitchen annex for the staff dining room, a storage room and a walk-in freezer. We built the children's comfortable apartment on the second floor, opening off a large sundeck. We could celebrate Christmas in privacy gathered around my Steinway piano. At the far end it was divided from our bedroom by an open hallway. When baby Lissa arrived she shared Mark's bedroom. Nancy and Lori's bedroom would soon need a plaque, reading, "YUL BRYNNER SLEPT HERE!"

Brynner arrived at the ranch during one of those holiday No Vacancy periods. The only space we could make available was to move Nancy and Lori in with us so he could have their room. Nancy remembered, "… going upstairs to make beds in my room, the weekend Yul Brynner was there. I knocked. There was no answer, so I walked in from the deck-side. And there he was with only a towel around his waist, shaving his head!"

He said, "Oh! Please come in," lowering his eyes and his voice.

"I didn't come in!"

Brynner felt right at home in our family unit, and made a practice of breakfasting with the staff before taking his morning ride. On their first evening at the ranch Yul and his wife Virginia introduced a new game, a brain-twister called Giotto, but it didn't catch on like Scrabble.

Our bedroom was directly above the kitchen, providing us with an "early warning system" for disasters below. If the crashing of pots and pans became deafening, it was a sure sign we were about to lose a chef.

Nearly completed SITA Headquarters wing gets some landscaping as Jack and Mitch Schaffer install a watering system for sholem ash tree planters.

September 1958
Helen Dengler Photo

64

One of my faithful SITA cyclists, Tom Dunnavan, was at the ranch when this happened. He saw gloom in my face.

"What's the matter, Helen?"

"Our chef just quit, Tom."

"Why don't you let me cook breakfast tomorrow?"

I wasted no time with questions and Tom took over.

At the table the next morning a chorus of voices asked, "Who's the new chef, Helen? We've had such a wonderful breakfast!" Tom had served them apple pancakes! I cornered him later to ask about his culinary background, and he just shook his head. "None whatsoever. I just look in a cookbook." He made it sound so easy!

As the years rolled by we adjusted to all the changes and improvements Jack implemented at the ranch, and welcomed them. In 1958, however, the next building project caused some upheavals. Moving Jack's SITA Travel Headquarters from New York's Fifth Avenue to White Sun was not going to please everyone. For Jack, the move consolidated SITA and White Sun operations in one spot, eliminating much of his commuting and allowing him more time with the family. But it caused dislocations for some SITA New York employees. Three key members were family men who thought the ranch a crazy idea and refused to move west.

Armin Lehmann was one SITA manager who accepted the move to the desert. "I was amazed!" was how he described White Sun. "It was absolutely captivating, the facility, the setting, the atmosphere … upscale but not pretentious. … A reflection of his [Jack's] character and symbolic of his accomplishments."

A smaller staff stayed on when SITA New York was downgraded to a regional office. Some moved away to other jobs. Jack had asked his Vice President and Controller, Regina Palevier, to move to the ranch. Regina was a workaholic, intensely loyal to Jack, coming in to the office early and staying late. New York had been her command post, and Regina ran a tight ship. An

The new SITA Headquarters wing is ready for a dramatic move from New York's Fifth Avenue to the desert. Quite a switch of pace!

October 1958
Paul Pospesil Photo

easterner, she was completely at home in the 24-hour turmoil of New York City. Her adjustment to life in the desert proved more difficult than mine.

The evening Regina arrived at the ranch, she found me playing games in the lobby with guests, and immediately jumped to her own conclusions. From then on she shadowed me. Regina was a confirmed teetotaler and sometimes during the "Happy Hour," she found me playing the bar piano, with a bottle of beer on the side. (So this is what Jack's wife is up to!) Regina didn't mingle. She disapproved. She had no time for frivolities and the "laid-back" White Sun life style. It was a foregone conclusion Regina would return to New York … and she did.

In May 1960, Shirley P. Jones became the bookkeeper at SITA's new head-quarters. Shirley was competent, "laid-back," good-natured, even-tempered, and a bright ray of sunshine. She fitted in!

Ramsay completed the first SITA office wing in 1959, built along the west side parking area. Like all subsequent additions, it matched the original White Sun units with the same, low, ranch-style porches, designed for easy conversion into future guest units. Jack prided himself on thinking ahead, but in this case, not quite far enough. SITA outgrew this new office in a couple of years.

An entirely new, expanded annex arose on "SITAPLATZ" closer to the stables. This time there was ample office space, telecommunications, and a large print shop. Additional rooms housed the growing SITA staff and overseas trainees. These trainees came to the ranch for thorough in-doctrination in Jack's methods before returning to various overseas SITA offices. They experienced something of a reverse culture shock upon returning home, accustomed as they had become to the ranch smorgas-bords, chuck wagon breakfasts, on-location riding stables, every kind of sport facility, and no need to commute anywhere!

SITA's White Sun Headquarters' staff also provided a bonus for guests, who enjoyed mixing with these bright, young foreigners, a regular "SITA United Nations." At one time or another, and during SITA Conferences, the ranch hosted overseas and domestic managers and staffers from the following cities, world-wide:

Historic portrait of SITA's "United Nations" team grouped around the patio fountain:

Standing from left: Hong Kong's Charlie Kwok; Bangkok's Prayong Somquamkid; Auckland's Roger Varcoe; Tokyo's Jon Ogawa; Athens' John Georgandas; New Delhi's Inder Sharma; Los Angeles' Jan Perry; Rancho Mirage Headquarters' John McDonald; Taipei's Robert Chu; Singapore's Chee Chye Tan; San Francisco's Lillian Martin; Houston's Del Calhoun; Melbourne's Charles Smith; Sydney's Warwick Gibson; and Seattle's David Dengler.

Seated from left: President Jack Dengler; Miami's Andre Ambron; Public Relations Director Helen Dengler; Manila's Jose Vicente Mapa; Cologne's Hilde Boker; Chicago's Armin Lehmann; Toronto's Alan Gibson; New York's John Crosby; and London's Malcolm Finighan

September 30, 1956
Paul Pospesil Photo

Executive Director Gordon Bain conducts a SITA managers' meeting in the Redwood Room, where New Zealand artist David Kennedy's art is on display.

November 1960
Lee Wenzlick Photo

*Postmaster Sid and Laura Greenleaf
thank Jack for the years of SITA mail-
ings that upgraded Rancho Mirage to
First Class status and a new post office.*

July 1962
Helen Dengler Photo

Africa: Cairo and Nairobi; Asia: Bangkok, Calcutta, Hong Kong, Jerusalem, Kyoto, Manila, New Delhi, Singapore, Srinagar, Taipei, Tel Aviv, Tokyo and Yokohama; Europe: Amsterdam, Athens, Cologne, Leiden, London, Madrid, and Paris; North America: Chicago, Houston, Los Angeles, Miami, New York, Rancho Mirage Headquarters, San Francisco, Seattle, and Toronto; Pacific: Auckland, Christchurch, Honolulu, Melbourne, Sydney and Tahiti.

Inder Sharma, SITA's India manager, headquartered in New Delhi, shared his memories of White Sun with me in his May 12, 2000 letter:

My first visit to White Sun Ranch was in 1955. I had no idea whatsoever, of Palm Springs or of the ranch, except for the fact that I was going to meet the wife of the Company President and owner. I dressed myself in an English tweed suit and a well starched white shirt. I took the train from Los Angeles, totally oblivious of the personality of the lady I was going to meet, the ambience of White Sun, and the informality of the people.

My first shock was when I got off the train ... no high rise platform ... one stepped down almost to ground level. I was the sole passenger alighting from the train. At the other end of the platform were two ladies, dressed in shorts, most informal, one of them even barefoot. A red-haired lady approached me while I was struggling with my heavy suitcase, welcoming me with a warm smile and a big hug. She was Helen Dengler and the barefooted lady was Jan Rouse. We drove in a convertible car. I had never felt so much out of place, but to the credit of these two young ladies, they never embarrassed me for my lack of knowledge of White Sun and its ambience and temperatures.

I had visualized a ranch to be a very large place with lots of cattle, horses and even expected to see some cowboys. White Sun was small. The credit for putting me at ease goes to Helen and Jan, and I was soon comfortable and ready for a swim, as even in the fall, the temperature was quite high. I spent two nights and was totally taken aback with the informality, homeliness and friendliness of the people.

Jack's proposed SITA Headquarters building to be located on Desert Air Hotel's runway, never materialized.

1966
Designed by Kenneth N. Lind

After 1956 until 1969, I must have made over two dozen trips to White Sun. My impressions kept improving, my feelings changing from that of a stranger to a member of the family, ... the few managers' meetings etched vividly in my memory. I still proudly display the last photograph of the Managers Meeting, where we posed as a group near the lily pond. White Sun grew from modest beginnings to a very large, sprawling, successful property, with a number of swimming pools, tennis courts and riding horses.

The barbecue dinners under the starlit nights, with beautiful people and the music and singing of Helen and Jack, ... vivid recollections of the Round-Up Bar, the dining area and the SITA offices. What lovely, lively and friendly evenings spent with charming people.

Jack wasn't going to be caught napping again, for SITA office space. In his memoirs he wrote:

I was considering a large, new SITA office at the front of the ranch, along the grass airstrip we shared with our neighbor, Desert Air Hotel.

He commissioned one of our ranch guests, architect Ken Lind to design the complex with

... a central rotunda, where my interest in astronomy came to the fore. I was planning to put in a planetarium and give astronomy lectures. I had a twelve-inch telescope at the ranch and a little planetarium unit, and gave frequent lectures for the guests.

Ken Lind, who had redesigned the ranch front entrance earlier, drew up some interesting sketches for Jack's futuristic SITA office. In the meantime rumors began circulating that Desert Air's owner, Hank Gogerty might be selling his place. If that happened the airstrip would disappear. Fortunately Jack abandoned the project. Desert Air Hotel did go on the market and is now owned and operated by Marriott Hotels. The airstrip was eliminated in favor of more hotel units.

Hidden away from the ranch guests behind a grapefruit orchard, the busy nerve center of Jack's world-wide travel network continued to thrive on White Sun's SITAPLATZ. During the '60s when SITA peaked, Jack foresaw a

74

shift in tourism coming, a shift from his original philosophy of educational, off-the-beaten-path tours to shorter, more conventional charter flight tours.

For some time Diners Club had been looking for a reputable travel wholesaler, to compete with American Express. Their final choice was SITA. After lengthy consultations, on April 28, 1968, Jack sold his 35-year-old SITA travel business to Diners Club. For the last time the ranch SITA office was dismantled. Like its predecessors it was transformed into additional ranch guest units. White Sun had started out with room for a dozen guests. Now it could accommodate 225!

During the early years SITA paid for the ranch expansion, before White Sun became financially independent. Now all that remained of its old supporter was the street sign SITAPLATZ.

Our repeat ranch guests provided plenty of eloquent testimony, but I was curious to know if White Sun had a wider reputation. David gave me an example. Attempting to make a left turn from a right lane while driving tourists to the airport, he was stopped by a Los Angeles police officer for a traffic violation. David remembered,

> The officer came around to my side of the car, to have a good look at me. Then he saw the White Sun sign on the door. "Oh, you're from the ranch!" he exclaimed. Then with a smile and a brief warning, he waved me on.

Another SITA member, Petie Ridgway joined me in San Francisco one evening for a symphony concert. Afterwards, as pre-arranged, we walked around to the stage door to greet some of the orchestra members we had met at the ranch. A guard barred our way.

Petie protested, "But Helen's from the ranch!"

This guard also smiled. "Well, why didn't you tell me so!" We were waved on through the stage door.

The ranch earned much wider recognition on the Perry Mason TV Show.[3] Hollywood was on the line when I answered the phone one day.

"Would it be possible, Mrs. Dengler, to bring our Perry Mason Show to the ranch for some background shots?"

I must confess my complete ignorance of that show, back then in the fifties. Confused, I repeated "The Perry Mason Show?" A staff member heard the magic words and whispered, "That's one of the best shows on TV, Helen."

I had more pressing matters on my mind and was about to hang up, but the agent persisted, assuring me White Sun would of course be reimbursed for any time and inconvenience. Reluctantly I agreed to set a date.

When the Perry Mason crew arrived, staff and guests turned out en masse to watch the action. They all knew who Perry Mason was!

A year went by and I heard nothing more until a letter arrived from our SITA office in far away Singapore, reporting what a thrill it had been to recognize White Sun on the Perry Mason Show! Many others have made similar reports, since, but even after fifty years of re-runs, I have yet to see that episode.[3]

★ ★ ★

White Sun's most unforgettable salute came from Air Force Major Dave Odell, a frequent ranch guest, during the height of the Cold War in the 1950s. On Odell's return from a distant S. A. C. mission, his huge B-47 Jet Bomber buzzed low over the ranch, throwing the whole valley into a panic, from Palm Springs to Indio. He told me much later, "I was so relieved to find White Sun still there!"

In those days the public was brain-washed with a relentless campaign to buy underground shelters, a vital safeguard, because of imminent atomic bomb attacks. Our local market, the Rancho Mirage Safeway Store displayed a portable shelter in its parking lot, ready for delivery. The public was urged to dig up backyards and bury the unit underground and then stock it for weeks to come.

A local photographer friend of mine, Paul Pospesil, credited with many of these White Sun photos, gave me a tour of his properly installed, underground backyard shelter. He had it stocked with enough canned goods and other staples to keep his family of four going for months. I thanked him for the tour and as I was leaving he said in all seriousness, "I'm sorry, Helen, but in case of an emergency, we won't have room to fit you in with us!"

I was given a scary look at White Sun's layout from the sky one afternoon, when an old SITA friend arrived. Andy Anderson, a member of my 1952 European bike tour, had flown in with a buddy landing on our neighbor's airstrip. On the tour Andy had been a challenge and a headache, a teenage smoker with a yen for whiskey and cigarettes but little energy or enthusiasm for bicycling. We slept in youth hostels on cycling days, where smoking and alcohol are strictly forbidden. Back then youth hostels only admitted individuals who arrived under their own power, on foot, bicycle, canoe or Faltboot. On two occasions Andy arrived by taxi! During the course of that two-month SITA tour, however, Andy turned over a new leaf, becoming a much healthier, cooperative member and even an enthusiastic cyclist!

Sauntering up to the White Sun desk to introduce his friend, Joe, Andy's reappearance took me completely by surprise. "How about taking a break for a few minutes, Helen? We'll fly you over the ranch and you can check it all out. Joe, here, is a wonderful pilot."

I thought about it. But they were insistent and persuasive. Finally this mother of six allowed Joe to buckle her into the back seat of a two-seater, open cockpit plane, with a wide seat belt so strong, I should have suspected what was coming!

"Just ask Joe if you have a problem, Helen." Those were Andy's parting words, shouted through cupped hands as we roared, full throttle into the blue.

Viewing White Sun from the sky, so peaceful, so neat and tidy, brought sudden tears to my eyes, and not because of the ferocious wind in my face. Joe gave me no time for a leisurely inspection of the ranch. Gaining altitude and speed, he dove into loops and belly rolls. I yelled into the wind with all my might, but to no avail. Joe just nodded his head and kept right on with his dazzling aerobatics.

78

Bird's-eye view of the rooftop of southern California, 11,502 foot Mount San Gorgonio at right and 10,805 foot Mount San Jacinto at left, that shelters the Coachella Valley. Rancho Mirage lies at its center, White Sun Guest Ranch at the foot of Desert Air Hotel's runway, in the foreground.

March 1959
United Aerial Survey Photo

79

What a weird sensation flying upside-down, the earth way above me! I had no feeling of standing on my head. That was what the world was doing! My heart pounding I wondered if I would ever plant my feet on it again.

Call it Andy's "revenge!"

I did live to plant my feet on earth again right side up, profoundly grateful to be back! During those harebrained minutes in the sky the ranch had suddenly grown very precious. I could never again take it for granted.

Jack's prophetic words came back to me, "You'll learn to love it, Helen!"

*Let's round up the redheads before
the twins leave for college: David 17,
Ian 14, Nancy 17, Mark 12, Lori 8, and
Lissa, the only brunette, going on 2.*

Summer 1955
Helen Dengler Photo

chapter 6
A Family Place

Jack was right all along. I did learn to love it. It just took me longer than our guests. They learned to love White Sun after one visit, having discovered it the perfect place to relax, to regain their sanity, to bring the kids, book a honeymoon, or celebrate family reunions. Family, that's what it was all about. White Sun was that safe haven they'd been searching for, a place where no one had to lock a door! There were so many activities and opportunities to meet wonderful new friends, why leave?

And that's precisely what people complained about. "The worst feature of White Sun," they claimed, "... is getting up the moral and mental fortitude to leave the darn place!"

One day driving south along Highway 111, Ruth and Cliff Powers from Pomona, noticed the sign that said, WHITE SUN GUEST RANCH. To investigate they turned off onto Magnesia Falls Drive. Two red headed boys were playing just outside the gate. Striking up a conversation with them, the Powers learned the boys were sons of the owners. Ian and Mark's version of life at White Sun intrigued them. "Let's give it a try!"

It didn't take many visits before the Powers became members of our extended family, returning year after year. They felt so at home they decided to share something special with us, an acorn from the big cork oak that grew in their Pomona front yard. Cliff planted it outside his White Sun room, where it grew tall and handsome.

Luring guests to the ranch was not part of the Dengler children's official job description. Their primary responsibility was to help keep the place neat and tidy. The four oldest redheads, David, Nancy, Ian and Mark, were each assigned a walkway or patio to sweep daily, before going to school. After school they were needed to fill in for dishwashers, maids or waiters. No need to ask if White Sun was a family place, with our

83

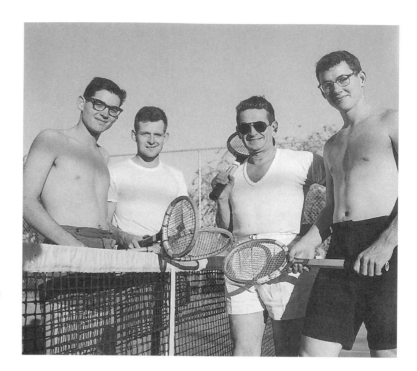

Papa Jack and the Dengler boys, Ian, David, and Mark, are ready to christen the first tennis court.

February 1957
Helen Dengler Photo

Long time White Sunners Cliff and Ruth Powers were introduced to the ranch by two small boys playing outside the big gate, Ian and Mark Dengler.

Fall 1953
Photo courtesy Cliff Powers

84

youngsters busy at work everywhere.

Building a warm sense of family was basic in Jack's business strategy. This proved invaluable in both his travel business and the guest ranch. (Well over half a century later, I'm still in contact with many old SITA members, as well as White Sun staff and guests.)

Jack's attitude towards his own family was more ambivalent. He loved his children, a source of wonder and delight when they were small. "Let's have some more, Helen!" But that chemistry changed as they grew up and developed strong personalities. He wanted them to follow in his footsteps as strong achievers, and that required serious discipline, about which I did not always agree. Being an absentee father much of the time did not help matters.

Jack's own father, John C. Dengler, Sr., was not his role model. Emigrating at the age of sixteen from Bruchsal, Germany to New York City, John Sr. had done very well in New York's brewery business, but he lost nearly everything in the Crash of 1929. Jack didn't go so far as to label his father a failure, but did consider him too easy-going, something he was never going to be!

And just a year before the disastrous stock market collapse, Jack's mother, Emma died. She had been caring for her favorite child, "Boysey" (Herbert), Jack's younger brother, ill with pneumonia. Boysey recovered but Emma contracted the disease, which proved fatal.

That left two teenage boys to be raised by Liesel Ziegler, Emma's supervising nurse from the hospital, who soon after became their stepmother when she married John Sr. The first time I met Liesel at the family's home in Jackson Heights, New York, I sensed an undercurrent of hostility at the dinner table. Liesel's nephew, Hans Ziegler, had also joined the family by then. Everyone seemed to be at odds with one another, which struck me as curious but hardly something to worry about.

In my family of seven there were plenty of arguments but never any question of our parents' love and devotion for each other and for each one of us. With all the confidence of youth I was sure I could straighten out any of Jack's family problems.

*Mark and Ian corner Lori in the game
room to practice domino strategy.*

February 1957
Paul Pospesil Photo

Puppeteers Lissa and Lori offer a preview of their Punch & Judy Show in front of the Rancho Mirage Post Office.

June 2, 1964
Helen Dengler Photo

Less than an hour's drive from White Sun's warm swimming pools, Christina McCandless, Lissa, and Emery Slocum indulge in a snowball fight.

Idyllwild, San Jacinto Mountains
January 1962
Helen Dengler Photo

88

"Watch me. Mom!" Lisa and her mother, Betty Kniesche, are all set for a work out in the swimming pool.

April 10, 1963
Helen Dengler Photo

Jack swings my office assistant Betty Ring at the Saturday night square dance.

December 1956
Lee Wenzlick Photo

90

The Burton family, Ed and his youngsters Marjorie, Bruce, and Barbara leave the ranch corrals and head for the sand dunes.

1965
Helen Dengler Photo

Chicagoan Ed Conrad tackles the pitch & putt golf course with brother-in-law Irvin Chase.

January 31, 1961
Paul Pospesil Photo

I genuinely loved John Sr., Jack's kindly, gentle father, an accountant and history buff, who enjoyed sketching and drawing medieval German towns. On the other hand Liesel was somewhat overpowering, especially when our children came along. Liesel was trained as a baby nurse. She had no children of her own and when we were together she tended to master mind the twins and my every move. After we moved to California, I was glad to have a whole continent between us!

Still in his teens and left with few resources during the Depression, Jack worked at a variety of jobs, his favorite as a caddie on Long Island golf courses. Not surprisingly, golf had to be included in White Sun's master plan, since the ranch happened to be in the very heart of "Golf Mecca," (where by 1999, over one hundred golf courses created a green belt, all the way from Palm Springs to Indio).

By 1958, Jack completed White Sun's 1000-yard, nine-hole Pitch & Putt golf course. This green expanse, framed by the Shadow Mountains, offered a pleasing view from the dining room windows. Trees scattered around the course included an assortment of young Aleppo pines, pepper trees, fan palms, and a magnolia tree.

Ian was assigned maintenance of the golf course during his high school days. He christened it "The Amazing Wonder of the South," adding in a recent conversation, "… it would take a Tiger Woods to play it!" The boundaries presented considerable hazards. Desert Air Hotel's landing strip ran along one side, where hooked balls frequently disappeared in the sand. Ian and his good friend, Stanley Little, collected a gold mine of abandoned golf balls from that runway.

The wash, a deep storm drain well camouflaged behind trees, ran below the opposite boundary line. Balls disappearing in that direction elicited the comment, "That must be a really big sand trap!" And at the far end of the course, more trees screened the ranch dump, where piles of tree trimmings and debris were burned. There were days when this hazard aided by the wind, created an impenetrable smoke screen.

Golf maintenance man Ian had more pet names. He called the large horseshoe-shaped water hole nearest the dining room windows, "The Icky Hole," because the ground around it was alive, "... for this was where all the toads in the desert came to have their babies!"

One player wagered the golf course must have been designed by the Marx Brothers! Frustrating or not, Jack's course offered great challenges!

At White Sun there was never a shortage of learning opportunities. One day an irate guest leaned over my office counter complaining, "My convenience is overflowing!" Mitch Schaffer was on call for such emergencies, and could provide us with a plumbing lesson. High up on White Sun's tower, David and Ian became nimble steeple-jacks, as well as painters, renewing the paint job on our landmark windmill. Our youngsters were a vital part of the White Sun staff.

Nancy elaborately decorated the dining room for birthday events and holidays. Every New Year she created individual crepe paper hats for each guest. Lori, and later, Lissa entertained Easter crowds with hilarious, handmade puppet shows. When the children were little, they were raised on my puppet shows, an art all the girls mastered, complete with original music, handmade papier-mâché puppets, and artistic stage settings.

With his big telescope, Jack introduced Mark to astronomy and the dazzling spectacle of the desert sky. Mark was happy to share this fascinating hobby with guests. One of his father's unfulfilled ambitions was to be the first man on the moon!

On square dance nights the boys mastered Harry Kester's calls, filling in for missing partners. Lori at age twelve, developed the annual Easter Horse Show for all the young riders. She was so in love with horses, she had to take hers along to college! Our scientist David introduced me to Magnesia Falls Canyon and the plight of the Bighorn Sheep.

With a setting like White Sun, the sky was the limit for creative parties. Any special occasion called for a celebration. Elaborate SITA Reunions honoring a different country each year, required a full year of research and preparation, and were staged as a fall opening for White Sun.

Repairs on the tower roof involve a challenging windmill paint job by steeplejacks Ian and David.

Fall 1952
Helen Dengler Photo

Everybody gets excited at Piñata parties in the ranch lobby that follow
New Year's Eve hayrides.

December 31, 1955
Jan Rouse Photo

As our six went off to college, each one chose to major in a different subject. They already had a head start in music, zoology, international and public relations, horsemanship, gamesmanship, geography, square dancing, gardening, history, biology, maintenance, drama, environmental awareness, and plumbing!

Whenever we had to turn people away on crowded holidays, they would ask us to recommend another family place just like White Sun.

"We're sorry. That doesn't exist."

Arthur Keleher had a soft spot for girls of all ages, including one-and-a-half-year-old Lissa Dengler.

April 1955
Helen Dengler Photo

chapter 7

King Arthur

"Reports of my Death Have Been Greatly Exaggerated"

How Arthur C. F. Keleher found his way from New York City to the White Sun, I can no longer remember, but it was a marriage made in heaven. White Sun's "Arthur Era" began in January of 1953. I was still a novice in the hotel business, still feeling my way. Arthur, on the other hand, was a long-time veteran of the Big Apple, and Palm Beach, Florida. He knew the hotel and resort business inside out, and he could size up guests the moment they walked in the door.

This was an art Nancy Carruthers had yet to learn. She was at the check-in desk the afternoon Arthur arrived. Carruthers had joined a SITA European bike tour in 1951, and like a number of other SITA travelers, had followed the Dengler family to apply for a job at the ranch.

Carruthers recalled, "I was sort-of in charge, and didn't want to make the decision to let Arthur stay. He looked like death warmed over, someone who wouldn't make it through the night. I suggested he return when Helen was here."

"But what a gem he turned out to be!"

Birthe Andersen, another staff member, as well as a SITA tour leader, also saw Arthur the day he walked in. "Marianne and I met him, and he took one look at us and decided if the ranch had such 'pretty girls,' it would be the place for him. Sometimes he would come into the dining room after dinner, when the staff had their coffee, and tell us stories, about when he was rich and his friends were the Hutton family, and he went sailing on their luxury yacht."

Arthur survived the "front desk test," and soon earned honored guest treatment. The ranch became his refuge from the "knife people" (surgeons).

*For his poolside office, Arthur claimed
the double bed mattress at right.*

April 1955
Helen Dengler Photo

He was fighting a losing battle with cancer, but was granted four winters' reprieve at White Sun.

It didn't take long for all of us, staff and guests alike, to discover Arthur's sterling qualities. He brightened our lives. He began by establishing his "office" on an old double-bed mattress beside the swimming pool. There he would sit and sun himself to his heart's content, while supervising the daily circus. His lean, tanned body, faded blue cap and glasses, became ranch fixtures. When the dinner bell rang, guests would vie for the privilege of sitting at his table, King Arthur at the head, dispensing a never-ending supply of wisdom and wit.

The ranch Round-Up Room became his five o'clock priority. It was just a private bottle bar during Arthur's reign, as it took us several years to secure a liquor license. One evening Arthur was seated on his pet bar stool, when an attractive young woman wandered in off the road. MGM star Biff Wilcoxon was acting bartender that night, and he offered her a complimentary drink. She thanked him and sat down next to Arthur, quietly sipping for a while. Then she turned to ask him, "Just what do you people do around here?"

Arthur studied her carefully, removed his cigarette, cleared his throat and finally responded in his raspy smoker's voice, "Well, we do nothing all day, and have a hard time fitting it all in."

One afternoon when Arthur was sitting in the lobby, an Iranian couple checked in, accompanied by the wife's brother. I could sense Arthur's hackles rising, as he studied the threesome. Later that same evening after the couple retired, the brother was left at loose ends, wandering listlessly around the lobby. Idly he fingered a backgammon board that had caught his eye.

"Anyone play backgammon around here?" The question was aimed at no one in particular. My assistant, Kathy Maclean, "the Green Pea" as she was known, a recent addition to the staff, happened to be in the lobby chatting with Arthur. Backgammon was his favorite game and he had found Kathy a quick learner.

"Why don't you show me the game?" Arthur challenged the fellow, a "rug boy" in Arthur's terminology. Arthur had a distinctive way with words.

The two gentlemen sat down facing each other at the backgammon table, and the Iranian began painstakingly explaining the rules. Arthur's face was a mask. He listened attentively, began playing slowly and won the first round. The Iranian beamed approval.

"You're doing very well, Sir!"

Arthur won the second game, the third game, and again, the fourth. His opponent was silent now.

"Why don't you teach this young lady the game?" Arthur nodded to Kathy, who had been watching intently. The Green Pea took Arthur's place at the table.

Now the fellow was irritable. He took on his new challenger with less enthusiasm and began the lesson all over again. Kathy won the first round. She won the second, but by the third, the gentleman stood up, declared he was sleepy, and abruptly left the lobby for his room.

The next morning all three checked out.

Arthur scored again at the Riverside County Fair and National Date Festival, since 1946 a colorful extravaganza held every February in nearby Indio, a railroad hub and center for Coachella Valley date ranchers. Dates thrived in the desert and were a major crop. This festival was famous. It was not only an annual county fair with exhibits of local produce, 4-H clubs, and prize animals. It included camel and ostrich races and a nightly Arabian Nights spectacle with fireworks. Spectators were entertained with dramatized tales from "A Thousand and One Nights," performed on a massive stage built to resemble a Moorish castle, golden towers, dancing girls and bearded viziers. Queen Scheherazade reigned over all.

Not surprisingly, Arthur was invited, in 1953, to serve as one of the festival's Queen Scheherazade Contest judges, along with Tony Szymanski, another SITA tour member and White Sun guest. They accepted with alacrity! What a lark for those 'brothers.' Arthur made no secret of his fondness for the fairer sex. Marianne (who would later become Mrs. Tony Szymanski), witnessed the judging, and recalls, "Both Tony and Arthur looked very serious, with their score-pads on their knees. I remember their ear-to-ear grins once

Solemn beauty contest judges Tony Szymanski and Arthur (center) mark their ballots, at the Riverside County Fair and National Date Festival held annually in Indio.

February 1953
Gilman Studio Photo

One beau and four belles all dolled up for a night on the town: Marianne, Birthe, Arthur, Helen, and Nancy Carruthers are heading for Palm Springs.

February 1953
Jan Rouse Photo

they cashed in on their 'fee,' a big kiss from the beauty contest winner!"

Marianne laughed about another evening date when Arthur invited four of us staffers to join him for dinner in Palm Springs, before his annual ranch departure in April. Formal attire at White Sun was a rare occurrence and casual informality the rule. Arthur rarely saw any of us in anything but shorts or slacks. Marianne explained:

"Carruthers, Birthe Andersen [a Danish tour leader], Helen and I made the laborious effort of struggling into nylons, skirts, high heels and gloves [please!] to be proper ladies, in response to Arthur's explicit request. It was definitely an elevating experience!"

Arthur inspired a remodeling job that transformed the White Sun interiors in the fall of 1955, although he was not destined to enjoy it. Our wooden dining room benches were too hard for his comfort. Likewise the sofa cushions in the lobby did not provide sufficient padding for his lean frame. Arthur needed a special pillow.

In Idyllwild, high above us in the San Jacinto Mountains, we discovered the Ted Belden Pinecraft Furniture workshop. His handcrafted, made-to-order pine tables, chairs, bedsteads, lamps, bookcases, headboards, any imaginable item, were ideal for the ranch.

Sadly, Arthur never witnessed the departure of the old, dilapidated furniture. It was all replaced with well-padded new sofas, a huge coffee table to match the big stone-walled fireplace, game tables, dining room chairs and tables, a pine-paneled game room, and bar stools in the Round-Up Room. New bedsteads, dressers and chairs were installed in the guest rooms, as well as small Pinecraft stools with White Sun engraved on the top, my favorites! One of these stools is still doing yeoman service in my vegetable garden in Montana.

★ ★ ★

During a personal crisis, Arthur came to my rescue. With each passing season as ranch manager, I had become less paranoid about the desert. As I learned to cope with my responsibilities, the challenge became more and more fascinating. In other words, I was "hooked." Jack could sense my

Ted Belden creates a "new look" for the lobby with his pinecraft furniture. Postmaster Sid Greenleaf chats with Eileen Bradwell, curled up on the new turquoise sofa.

Fall 1955
Clemens of Copenhagen Photo

Arthur and Bella Bella are good companions. For 35 years, dachshunds were always part of the Dengler family.

1954
Helen Dengler Photo

107

transformation and determination to succeed. At White Sun, work hours came close to around-the-clock, at times, which Jack considered a detriment to "my raising the family."

It had taken him five years to dislodge me from Santa Barbara, but now, that goal achieved, was he having second thoughts?

SITA President and world traveler Jack, who left thousands of tourist dollars in his wake, enjoyed red carpet treatment wherever he went. Returning to White Sun was something of a letdown. Guests were number one at the ranch, the rightful recipients of red carpet treatment, weekends, holidays, mornings, or late hours in the bar. It took some ingenuity to fit in private family life.

But this was a challenge I enjoyed, and Jack's unwelcome comments about "my raising the family" or neglecting the kids, were becoming sore points. Just who was doing the neglecting? Busy rebuilding SITA's postwar travel business, exploring and expanding tours to new destinations, Jack touched base at the ranch only briefly between his global flights. Some guests had never set eyes on papa Jack, and wondered about all those Dengler kids!

As a matter of fact a sixth Dengler was on the way in 1953.

Keen observer Arthur stepped into the breach, sensitive as always. He had no intention of accepting a change in White Sun management. I had confided in him when Jack suggested, out of the blue, "Wouldn't you like to move back east, Helen? We could find a house somewhere in Connecticut?"

Arthur managed to corner Jack one day. "You know, Jack, this ranch means a great deal to Helen. She's doing her best to please you, and to see that White Sun continues to thrive. You have entrusted her with the job. Let her do it."

I heard no more talk of Connecticut.

All my doubts and imagined horrors of the desert were evaporating. Just as Jack had predicted back in 1946, I was falling in love with the desert and my job, confident now I could master it. Ranch guests were a delight, opening up new worlds, and it was rubbing off on the children. I was discovering extraordinary adaptations of flora and fauna in this harsh environment, its subtle beauty, this strange, yet ancient world of purple mountains and sand verbena. Surely I, too, could adapt?

As the desert heat intensified in April, it was time to drive Arthur down to Indio, for his train ride back to New York, and his comfortable 48th Street Eastside apartment, where his devoted friend Evelyn looked after him. During that first winter at the ranch he had already won our hearts, and had become the most cherished guest of all. His letters attest to the fact that Arthur, too, was hooked on White Sun.

November 30, 1953:

Helen Dear,

Hold on to your sombrero. If you will have me and can get your kitchen cabinet to pass favorably on me, as a member in good standing, you have a customer. I hope to hear OK from you, which will make me very happy. Might keep this as a surprise for the G I R L S.

Devotedly, Arthur

December 12, 1953:

My Dear Helen,

Pucker up sisters, come Tuesday, the 15th, the brother will be on his way, and will be looking for a smiling face at 12:57 P.M., Friday the 18th, at the Southern Pacific Indio station.

January 20, 1955:

Planning to arrive in Indio, January 31st. So you will know me, I'll be wearing a blue shirt and you wear your red hair and a beam in the eyes … I am thinner, with more rubber in my legs, but I hope my bits and pieces will hold together.

Arthur's farewell party filled the dining room to capacity, including ardent fans Jan Rouse, Ruth Powers, Ed Wetterstrom and Helen.

April 14, 1953
Nancy Carruthers Photo

So you see, Helen, you have twisted my arm … you have always made a monkey out of my heart.

With affection,
Arthur

Arthur's letters were always a treat, full of questions and good advice for the staff and guests, and especially, for girls on the prowl. "If the carom shot fails, try a picnic, but make it good. I am a pushover for a picnic."

Marianne described Arthur's final ranch visit. "His last year was already overshadowed by his throat cancer. Normally he was the first in for breakfast, checking out the best bacon with his morning coffee and paper. As he grew weaker, we in the kitchen suggested breakfast-in-bed. He smiled and accepted! When we included a fresh flower on his tray, it nearly choked him with a little emotional tear."

"Isn't it funny how he tried to figure us all out [and most of the time he did], but nobody really knew him or anything about his past! From the staff to the visitors, nothing escaped his eagle eye. … I think he genuinely loved us all."

For years previous to his arrival at White Sun, Arthur had been living on borrowed time. His name had appeared in the book, THE LAST RESORT as, "… the late Arthur Keleher." This was a great joke among his many fans and friends. His courageous fight against cancer ended March 11, 1956, in New York City. As a veteran Army Captain in the First World War, his body now lies in Arlington Memorial Cemetery, in Washington, D.C.

At White Sun he lives among the immortals.

Madame Bobbie (Mrs. Robert Winkel-stroeter) tackles anything with enthusiasm, from the labyrinth of the Tokyo subway system, to White Sun's golf course on a riding mower.

March 1958
Helen Dengler Photo

chapter 8
Tahiti's Madame Bobbie

I first met Jeanie Winkelstroeter in a tiny Tokyo tempura bar, when I was attending a PATA Conference (Pacific Area Travel Association), in 1956. I took an instant shine to her. She was just one of those people you feel you have known all your life. Jeanie paid a visit to White Sun two years later during a promotional tour for her company, Air Tahiti and Tahiti Tours. She was known as Madame Bobbie[1] in Tahiti, since Mrs. Robert Winkelstroeter was much too complicated for the natives to pronounce. Jack had known her since his first exploratory visit to Tahiti, in 1955.

"Now it's your turn to come and visit my island, Helen," she smiled, "and observe what happens during our exciting 14th of July Bastille Day celebrations!" What an invitation! How I longed to say yes!

Back in the 1930s Bobbie had acquired a copra and vanilla plantation on Tahiti's neighboring island of Moorea, twelve miles distant across a rough channel. As a French citizen she was entitled to buy land in French Oceania. She and her German husband wanted no part of pre-war Europe and had settled on this remote spot in the South Pacific to raise their three children.

113

In 1939, since Bobbie's husband was German, and France was at war with Germany, he was interned during the war years on a tiny immigration isle in Papeete's harbor. That left Bobbie and the children isolated on her large plantation in Moorea. There were few whites on the island, and certainly no doctor.

One day a local Tahitian called on Bobbie for help. His cow had taken sick. Obligingly she consulted a veterinary book which happened to be on her library shelf, and then accompanied the man home. She saved his cow. Several weeks later the man returned, again asking for help. This time his wife was sick and would she please come? Bobbie protested she was not a doctor, not even a nurse. The man smiled patiently and waited for her to come. She shrugged her shoulders and once again accompanied him home. She had saved his cow. She would save his wife, and she did.

Word spread. In the years that followed, Bobbie safely delivered twenty-three babies!

With the world at war, Tahiti's copra export business languished. Bobbie had to think of alternatives. There was a market for grass skirts among servicemen and when popular Panama hats disappeared, Bobbie taught the natives how to make pandanus hats.

During his internment, Bobbie's husband passed the time reading Indian philosophers, and decided to become a yogi. When he was finally released, he was so fed up with Tahiti, he left to establish permanent residence in India.

But Madame Bobbie had become firmly rooted in the islands. She studied every book and record she could unearth on Polynesian life and culture, becoming fluent in the Tahitian language and gaining the natives' trust. Aging chiefs shared their wisdom and folklore with her, and by degrees she became an outstanding authority and champion of the Tahitian way of life.

When Bobbie encouraged me to visit her in Tahiti, the odds against it seemed insuperable. I had too many responsibilities, including ranch manager, tour leader, and my six children, ages four to nineteen. How could I persuade Jack to reverse roles and take over my job? He was forever on the go developing his thriving SITA travel business.

Jack had already signed me up to conduct a European summer bicycle tour. On May 26th, 1958, I wrote him:

"I didn't ever believe that you really wanted me to accept Jeanie's invitation. You don't believe in holidays—only holidays for SITA clients. Of course you know I will go to Europe and will love being with a student bike group again. But I shall also dream about Bastille Day with Jeanie."

My resourceful ranch assistant, Lynn Morgan had a plan. She whisked me off to Palm Springs on a shopping spree, to help me select a suitable wardrobe for the Matson Line cruise to Tahiti. Then she paraded me, all dolled up, in front of Jack.

"Don't you think she looks great, Jack, for a South Seas holiday?"

Lynn kept up this banter, as if my departure were a foregone conclusion. Yet right up to the last moment, even after Jack cancelled my European tour assignment, even after he had confirmed bookings for me, Tahiti still seemed out of reach, so remote it was surely a fantasy.

When I actually had my feet firmly planted on the deck, at the S. S. MONTEREY's railing, and was waving goodbye to my family on the Matson Line pier, I knew it was a miracle. I could see water widening a gap between us! This was a first for me, no tour group in tow, no children, no guests, no responsibilities! And I didn't know a soul on board.

Alone at last, I withdrew to the elegant privacy of my cabin, enjoying the comfortable bed overtime, becoming an uncooperative, antisocial passenger, much to the bewilderment of the eager cruise director. Now at last there was unlimited time to revel in the ship's well-stocked library, devouring books on Tahiti and the South Seas. The dining room served marvelous food. No phone calls, no laments from guests or children!

Every now and then there were restless periods when I felt this can't be real. I MUST DO SOMETHING! But I stifled the urge.

115

The S.S. MONTEREY'S captain orchestrated the most perfect climax to our eight-day cruise, with a dawn sighting of Tahiti. Oh that breathless moment when a magical isle materializes on the horizon! Clouds hid the lofty peaks, a sure sign of land in these vast reaches of the Pacific. Can anything compare with the majesty of a ship bearing down on land, misty clouds furling themselves to reveal violet-green mountainsides, pinnacles of blue against a golden sea? The film MUTINY ON THE BOUNTY had been screened the night before, to heighten our anticipation, and now I could almost see billowing sails over head, and bearded pirates at the railings.

Tahiti is the principal island and residence of French Polynesia's governor. This vast, watery domain, almost as large as Europe, spreads over one and a half million square miles of ocean. The total land area of 118 islands and atolls covers only 1500 square miles, varying from towering volcanic peaks to low coral atolls. Tahiti itself consists of two almost circular land areas, joined by a narrow isthmus. Its highest peak towers 7688 feet, dropping precipitously through lush vegetation to the narrow, fertile coastal plain. An almost continuous coral reef protects the shoreline, broken at intervals to form natural ship channels.

Far-famed, colorful Papeete is the capital, and back in 1958 it was relatively unspoiled. The jet airport, offshore over the water, was only in the planning stages at that time. Transportation to the island was infrequent, occasional cruise ships calling, and usually a seaplane bringing mail and a few passengers every fortnight. Life moved at a slow, even pace to match the daily six o'clock rising and setting of the sun. Tahiti lies a little closer to the equator than Hawaii, the former to the south and the latter to the north.

Tahiti's companion island Moorea of Bali Hai fame, lies to the west across a twelve-mile channel. Smaller and more primitive, Moorea was to become my hideaway, my escape to paradise. This time paradise did not elude me!

As soon as the S.S. MONTEREY docked in Papeete's magnificent harbor, Madame Bobbie came bouncing on board, greeting me with a flower lei. She began by apologizing, "I have a lot of business with the ship in port. Would you mind waiting?"

Would I mind waiting? In Tahiti? I stood spellbound on the beach, struggling to digest it all, the animated waterfront, yachts from every corner of the world bobbing at anchor, right before my eyes.

Suddenly I felt a gentle pressure against my legs. A Tahitian lady had shoved an old crate under me, so I could sit down to absorb the scene in a proper manner. As if we were old acquaintances, she began chatting in the slow, easily understood French all the natives spoke. I asked her where she came from and her answer almost convinced me I was in the land-of-make-believe. "Pitcairn Island!" She had stepped right out of MUTINY ON THE BOUNTY.

If only she had thought to bring along some pampelmous (grapefruit) from her backyard! She promised to give me some next time. Next time? She never stopped chatting until Bobbie came to fetch me. Then with a little wave she departed, "Hare oe, Parahi,"—"You go, I stay," the classic Tahitian goodbye.

By a strange coincidence I did meet that same lady again in a market, the day I was flying home. With a pleasant smile she resumed the conversation exactly where we had broken off six weeks earlier!

Since Bobbie was Tahiti's mastermind, we had to put off our visiting while the cruise ship was in port. She not only represented airlines, travel agents, and operated Tahiti Tours, but in her spare time she coached the Tahitians, helping them revive their ancient dancing rituals, singing and drumming. In addition she was building Aimeo, a resort hotel with bungalows, on the neighboring island of Moorea. And Moorea was to be my ultimate destination.

Meanwhile I was a guest in Bobbie's comfortable Papeete home, joining her for coffee breaks at her favorite waterfront café, overlooking Papeete's busy harbor. The café's outdoor veranda served admirably as Bobbie's office and conference room in this town of 18,000, where she knew almost everyone, and they always knew where to find her.

One morning over coffee, we were chatting with Monsieur Abel and a friend, when they excused themselves for another appointment. "But Helen can drive you," Bobbie offered, handing me the keys to her compact little

Renault. So I climbed into the driver's seat and the two gentlemen folded themselves into the narrow back seat.

Papeete's harbor area seethes with bodies, completely blocking traffic. My "fares" had mentioned an 11:30 appointment, and it was now almost twelve. I edged the car cautiously into the milling throng and honked for right of way. That caused a sudden, stunned silence everywhere. Voilà, the "Ugly American!" Cars have no right-of-way here, only pedestrians! My passengers were obviously embarrassed by their rude chauffeur. In Tahiti nobody seemed in a hurry.

Relax, I told myself! You are in Tahiti. The gentlemen should have walked!

Back home we consider ourselves "civilized," but I was rapidly learning a new meaning to that word!

Bobbie broadened my education some more that evening, when she took me to a village some distance away, for a dance rehearsal. Darkness falls like a velvet curtain at six o'clock every night, so the natives illuminate outdoor activities with flaming torches. In a forest clearing about the size of a baseball field, men and women in grass skirts were rehearsing for the coming Bastille Day competitions. Watching over children, grandparents were seated on the ground, forming a circle all around the dancers. From wee toddlers to teenagers, the children imitated the sinuous hip movements of the dancers with flawless accuracy.

Occasionally Bobbie would step forward for a conference with the head chief, demonstrating a movement in the dance. At first the chief would try it out with much laughter and clowning, but he soon made it part of the routine, adopting it as his own.

Before we could leave for Moorea, Bobbie kept me busy digesting the reference material and art books at her Papeete home and exploring the island on her bicycle. Once her business was completed, we could embark on l'Oiseau des Isles, a large boat that crossed the channel to the island and Bobbie's Aimeo Hotel, on Cook's Bay. After we stepped on board, an elderly gentleman followed us, wearing a wide-brimmed pandanus hat, crowned with a spectacular flower lei. The delicate white blossoms, Tiara

Tahitian hula dancers' sinuous hip gyrations are mastered as soon as a toddler can walk. Grass skirts are first bleached with lime juice and later dyed yellow, red or blue. A small gardenia, Tiare Tahiti, adds an elegant touch to their costumes.

Aimeo Hotel
July 1958
Helen Dengler Photo

119

My little grass shack was paradise for six weeks.

Aimeo Hotel, Moorea
July 1958
Helen Dengler Photo

120

Tahiti, dew-fresh and deliciously fragrant, gave the old man a stylish elegance noticed by all the passengers. The captain eyed the hat and immediately began showering the owner with compliments. In accordance with Tahitian custom, the old fellow removed the lei and presented it to the captain.

Bobbie, whose eyes missed nothing, whispered in my ear, "Just wait, Helen." When we disembarked, she sidled up to the captain with her own brand of flattery, and was soon in possession of the beautiful lei. Once ashore in Moorea, she placed it around my neck, explaining that anything you admire in Tahiti, even another man's wife, becomes your property!

But I wondered, ... for how long?

In a letter to my family I described my arrival in Moorea.

Tiara Tahiti (gardenia)
Anonymous Photo

The sun shone on lush, green mountainsides and the foremost row of jagged peaks. Waves broke over the coral reefs well offshore, and the colors inside the reef defy description, but I'll try. Azure, opal, and black sand alternating with pure white beaches. Below jagged cliffs, the land tapers off in a pattern of lava flows, to the palm-fringed coastal plain.

There's very little level land, only a small percentage of the whole island. Coconut palms, mixed with ironwood, breadfruit and hibiscus trees with yellow blossoms, bananas, papaya, and more. The cultivation of fruit trees, bamboo, vanilla and coffee takes place in interior valleys. There is so much more to see and learn!

Bobbie's Aimeo Hotel is not the Hilton. It was built at the usual leisurely Tahitian pace because Tahitians don't care much for serious jobs. The government provides them with land, and nature's bounty takes care of most of the rest. But they work for Bobbie! Aimeo's roofs are thatched, a Polynesian style she has revived, convincing the natives to give up the

121

tin roofs the colonials preferred, for the cooler thatch, using native materials.

Aimeo's main building is a faithful copy of a Polynesian Longhouse, roofed with pandanus leaves, a deep fringe hanging below the eaves, supported by peeled coconut trunks, polished and lacquered to a bright glaze. Entrance posts carved in the native manner, are reminiscent of our northwest coastal Indian totem poles. Everything is up-to-date, however in the spacious kitchen, and modern plumbing in the bathrooms. Don't look for hot water! A cool shower is always refreshing in the year-round balminess of the tropics.

The prize is my own, private, thatched little house on stilts, perched over the water. Through the wide cracks in the floor boards, I can watch a rainbow parade of tropical fish swim by, and on some mornings hear the soft voices of fishermen.

Now my challenge was to learn how to relax. Bobbie told me to sit under a coconut palm and empty my mind. Sound easy? Weeks later when it was almost time for me to fly home, I was just beginning to get the hang of it!

In the meantime preparations for Bastille Day filled the air with the Tahitian beat, furious, staccato dance rhythms, that ended with no warning, no slackening of the pace, just a jarring, abrupt halt, before starting anew. Dance groups, choirs and outrigger canoe teams rehearsed everywhere, with that throbbing beat filling the night. Delirious excitement!

Bobbie knew my classical music background, and asked me one day if I was getting tired of Tahitian music. "Would you like to hear some chamber music, Helen?"

She was always surprising me, but this was a stunner, almost impossible. Chamber music instruments wouldn't stand a chance in this humid environment. I nodded my head and waited to see what would happen.

After sundown, we went to visit a friends' home. Entering the breezy living room, I couldn't miss the commanding presence of a grand piano. Its legs were planted in kerosene tins to discourage insects, with light bulbs attached underneath the instrument to lessen the humidity. Our host leaned over the piano to tune a few sour notes, before the concert began. The musicians, all European refugees like Bobbie, opened with a Mozart trio, transporting me far away to the familiar world of classical music. I marveled at their artistry. A Beethoven quartet followed, and then the pianist turned to me.

"Madame Dengler, I understand you are a composer. Won't you play something for us?"

Startled, I moved over to the piano and played a song I had composed for our youngest daughter, Lissa.

> Lissa is a little girl,
> Everybody knows.
> She's a Dengler through and through
> From her head down to her tippy toes.

As I left the bench, the pianist slipped into my place, and without missing a beat, improvised at least fifteen variations on my Lissa theme song. These truly were musicians!

Bobbie was always full of tales and shared this story of shrimp poachers with me.

During the war food was sometimes a problem, even on this tropical isle. Shrimp were available in the stream that flowed through her plantation, but poachers were robbing her bounty. Bobbie well knew how fearless Tahitians were, above and below water, handling flaming dance torches, or walking barefoot over hot lava. She also knew how superstitious they were about powerful "spirits" they believed dwelt in the dark forests and mountain regions of the island's interior.

Improvising one night, she dressed up as one of those "spirits," decking herself out in a white sheet and mask. She perched on a rock, jutting high above the stream bed, and waited. Hearing voices, she lit a great, flaming torch and let out a wild cry.

That was the last time she had poachers.

One day I borrowed a bicycle to visit Bobbie's neighbors, an American couple, Medford and Glad Kellum. Their plantation was about a mile away, also on Cook's Bay. Med had a world-class shell collection, on which he was an authority. The Kellum's children and Bobbie's three had all grown up together on the island. Their parents assumed they would teach each other French and English. Overhearing them at play, the children were speaking Tahitian, of course!

Bobbie's eldest daughter, Crista, had mastered every sinuous twist of the Tahitian hula with such perfection, I urged Bobbie to let her visit us at White Sun for the SITA Tahitian Reunion, already in the planning stage. Since Crista had chosen a career in the hotel industry, why not let the ranch serve as part of her education? I prevailed and Crista arrived at White Sun. Tall and blond she dazzled us all, not only with her barefoot dancing but with expert mechanical skills. En route to the airport at the end of her desert visit, my station wagon blew a tire. Without hesitation she insisted, "Let me do this!" She found the necessary tools, jacked up the car and changed the tire in nothing flat.

Among other wondrous things, life in Tahiti is a great training ground!

My South Seas holiday came to an end with Bastille Day. There would be no leisurely cruising home. This time I flew out by seaplane. As we took off, spraying cascades of water over the waves, all I could hear was the Tahitian beat throbbing in sync with the plane's roaring motors. The sounds of all those bongos, pahus (hollow logs), toeres (wood blocks), bamboo drums, guitars and nose flutes that had echoed through the island for weeks, along with the lovely himenes (oral history sung in four-part harmony), were rudely shattered when we landed at Fiji's Suva Airport. The blaring, piped-in music was unmistakably American jazz!

Friends from Tahiti, Glad and Medford Kellum come to White Sun for a reunion with Glad's brother, Reginald Laughlin, at left.

March 6, 1960
Paul Pospesil Photo

At the ranch Bobbie's daughter Crista Winkelstroeter demonstrates the Tahitian hula for White Sunners Jan Makafske and Mary Nelson.

December 1959
Helen Dengler Photo

126

An accomplished rider at eleven, red-headed Lori's dream comes true, a horse of her very own, Rusty!

May 1958
Helen Dengler Photo

chapter 9
Wranglers & Riders

A guest ranch means horses. We worked out a deal with Henry Arnaiz, from Idyllwild, to lease his string of horses during the winter months, the desert's busiest season. Nestled in the piñyon pines six thousand feet above the desert floor, Idyllwild is a popular summer resort in the San Jacinto Mountains. You can swallow an entire geology lesson driving up the steep, winding curves of Highway 74 to get there, climbing through five distinct life zones, from Sonoran Desert to Arctic Alpine. In summer the place blossoms with camps, summer schools and other recreational activities. Not so, in winter. Our stable owner was happy to know his horses would be active, cared for, and well fed down at White Sun.

When the ranch bell announced breakfast, wrangler Al Hein would come into the dining room with his pad and pencil to sign up riders. Afterwards, down at the corrals, he matched each rider with the right horse. Whenever I could get away, he'd sign me up, too. Having survived my indoctrination with Black Hawk in the Palm Springs Western Week Parade, I'd learned to enjoy riding, with five-year-old Lori held close in front of me. That was her horse indoctrination, and the beginning of her transformation into a dedicated horse person.

Jack insisted I needed extra help, with our sixth and last little Dengler due in February 1954. Bill and Fran Paulson, popular managers of the Catalina Guest Ranch, came for our winter season. Their ranch was a much favored summer resort on Catalina Island, about thirty-three miles off the southern California coast. Our new co-managers arrived with their youngest daughter, Jan.

They also brought along SCRABBLE, a new game which they shared with us one evening. Bill and Fran's fascination with this game spread like wildfire at the ranch.

SCRABBLE is introduced by Fran and Bill Paulson, our 1953–1954 managers. Nancy Carruthers and Kathy Maclean are cogitating over their next move.

November 1953
Eddie Carroll Photo

Jan Paulson was born with hip problems that retarded her ability to walk. Her parents discovered there was a middle step, when they placed the little girl on a horse. She could ride! She rode before she could walk. Her doctor recommended a dry climate and White Sun was just the ticket.

Jan Paulson's love affair with horses infected Lori, who eagerly picked up all the tricks Jan taught her. Never short on ambition, Lori was soon riding the most spirited horses in the ranch corrals. One Easter holiday the Levensaler family arrived. Lori met Gale Levensaler, also a rider, and they became fast friends. The girls agreed they would never grow fat or tall, so they could both become jockeys!

Lori began participating in neighborhood horse shows, gradually collecting prize ribbons. What she lacked was a horse of her very own. In the fall of 1957, I wrote to a former ranch guest for advice: "Our ten-year-old Lori lives only for horses. We are now looking for an animal to buy ... The suspense is so terrible, Lori is having difficulty breathing! The consensus of opinion seems to be a horse around six or seven years old, gentle, but with spirit, since she is a good little rider."

Our search found Rusty. Unfortunately Rusty didn't measure up to Lori's expectations. In due course he was replaced by Lori's beloved mare, Coffee, half quarter horse and half thoroughbred.

Easter was the biggest draw of all the desert holidays, when the ranch overflowed with children heading for the corrals. To keep them busy, when Lori and her buddy Gale were both age 12, they inaugurated the White Sun Easter Horse Show. In the shade of the pepper trees that lined the east side of the ranch arena, they set up a judges' table, bedecked with colorful blue, red and yellow ribbons, for first, second and third place in Horsemanship and Demonstration. Nearly everyone got a prize!

Lori credits Colonel Fagan, her riding master at Kennolyn Camp, for her invaluable training in horsemanship. Nestled in the Santa Cruz mountains near Soquel, California, and founded by former SITA members Max and Marion Caldwell, Kennolyn was, and still is, a unique and wonderful camp for kids. Lori enjoyed several summers as a Kennolyn camper and I joined her there as a music counselor in 1960.

Lori and Gale Levensaler, originators of the Easter Horse Show, ride off bareback on Rusty.

Easter 1959
Helen Dengler Photo

"Your attention, please! The winners!" Lori awards ribbons during her seventh annual Easter Horse Show, assisted by Linda Hardesty, to the right of the prize table.

April 16, 1965
Paul Pospesil Photo

Eager horse show contestants await turns: Jody Serling, Nora Sargent, Bruce Burton, Julie Chester, Carla Howard, and Barbara Burton.

April 16, 1965
Paul Pospesil Photo

Rod Serling, of "Twilight Zone" fame, was so impressed with Lori's Easter Horse Shows in which his daughters, Jodie and Nan, won ribbons in Junior Horsemanship, that he drew up the following Resolution!

A RESOLUTION

For Miss Laurie Dengler from the White Sun Family

WHEREAS: You have given so unstintingly of time and effort to arrange and execute our Annual Horse Show, and

WHEREAS: You have unselfishly taken time out from personal vacations so as not to disappoint our young equestrians, and

WHEREAS: You have, year after year, with both efficiency and dedication, personally taken charge of this exciting event,

BE IT RESOLVED THAT THE GUESTS OF WHITE SUN OFFER TO YOU THEIR THANKS, APPRECIATION AND AFFECTION. THE BIG BLUE RIBBON GOES TO LAURIE!

Signed and attested to, this
16th day of April, 1965,
BY EVERYONE!

The horse show arena was a good example of Jack's planning. When he laid out the first tennis court in 1956, a windbreak was vital to protect the court from becoming a large sand-pile, desert winds being unpredictable and frequent. Staff and Dengler children transplanted tamarisk tree roots in an irrigation ditch along the west border. These hardy trees need little encouragement, and the border grew into a dense, twenty-foot tall windbreak.

Development fever was overtaking the desert, with bulldozers laying waste the beautiful Coachella Valley date groves, to make way for golf courses and condominiums. Full-grown date palms flooded the market.

A RESOLUTION —

FOR MISS LAURIE DENGLER
FROM THE WHITE SUN FAMILY

WHEREAS YOU HAVE GIVEN SO UNSTINTINGLY OF
TIME & EFFORT TO ARRANGE & EXECUTE
OUR ANNUAL HORSE SHOW, AND

WHEREAS YOU HAVE UNSELFISHLY TAKEN TIME
OUT FROM PERSONAL VACATIONS SO AS
NOT TO DISAPPOINT OUR YOUNG EQUESTRIANS,
AND

WHEREAS YOU HAVE YEAR AFTER YEAR WITH BOTH
EFFICIENCY & DEDICATION, PERSONALLY TAKEN
CHARGE OF THIS EXCITING TRADITIONAL EVENT

BE IT RESOLVED THAT THE GUESTS OF
WHITE SUN OFFER TO YOU THEIR THANKS,
APPRECIATION & AFFECTION. THE BIG
BLUE RIBBON GOES TO LAURIE!

SIGNED & ATTESTED TO
THIS 16th DAY OF APRIL, 1965

BY EVERYONE!

"Twilight Zone" producer Rod Serling, whose two daughters participated in the Horse Shows, penned a "Resolution" for Lori and sealed it with blood from his cut finger!

May 1961
Helen Dengler Photo

135

*Puddles from a sudden deluge mirror
newly transplanted date palms as well
as small spectator Lissa.*

February 1957
Helen Dengler Photo

Born a New Yorker but at heart a western pioneer, Jack rides his favorite mount, a tractor!

April 1958
Helen Dengler Photo

Jack Dengler Rides Again

Oh sound the cymbal, beat the drum
The White Sun chariot has come!
Behold the master of each gear:
It's Jack, the White Sun Charioteer!

What has his mighty monster done,
As o'er the desert sand it's run?
What feats of strength, what awesome power,
That causes desert land to flower?

Great trees are felled and pulled away,
And palms are planted, here to stay;
Waving their graceful fronds on high
A rhythmic pattern across the sky.

Ditches are dug and pipes are laid,
So links are green and flowers bathed.

Whence came the trenches and who laid—
The endless conduits that made—
A glow, which etches palms with light,
Shining beacons in the night?

The chariot roars and shifts its gears,
And lo, the darkness disappears!

The charioteer dismounts and smiles
An end to work, an end to trials.

So hail the Chief and hail his Steed!
A toast to both, in wine and mead.

Hail White Sun Chariot!

Roblay McMullen

137

Jack soon had a double row gracing the west border, grapefruit trees interplanted with the date palms, doubling the tamarisk windbreak. This still left a large open area between the windbreaks and the tennis court.

Jack's favorite mount was his tractor. It dug the ditches for a grid of irrigation pipes to water another tie-down device, a field of alfalfa that would fill in the open area. The alfalfa flourished, and soon needed cutting. Jack ventured into the cattle business. Several sets of calves became Lori's bottle-fed babies and alfalfa-mowers.

"But please, Daddy, they're not for Steak Fries! Why not make the alfalfa field a horse show arena?"

So be it. We had to sell the calves to out-of-town buyers. Lori won out and the alfalfa field was converted into an arena.

Lori knew her mare Coffee was special and she was eager to breed her. So be it, again! In due course on April 21, 1964, Coffee gave birth to Huckleberry, a splendid colt. This much-anticipated event took place only days after the Easter crowd checked out, much to the disappointment of children who had gone home.

Lori's horizons broadened dramatically following her graduation from Indio High School. Horse-related activities took a back seat. Raised in the SITA family tradition, she embarked on her first SITA European Bicycle Tour as a foreign correspondent for PALM DESERT ENTERPRISE, the local paper. As soon as she returned from Europe she was off to college and a plunge into the 1960s student turmoil at the University of California Berkeley campus.

During that chaotic period of student rebellion, Lori's colt, Huckleberry went on his own rampage, the only stallion in the White Sun stables. We had purchased the ranch donkey Jezebel, from Andy the Donkey Man, who kept his string of donkeys up on the highway for kids to ride. Everyone loved Jezebel. One day we discovered that sweet, gentle Jezebel was expecting!

Was this a conspiracy hatched up by the wranglers?

*Andy the Donkey Man, remembered
with great affection by many.*

February 1958
Helen Dengler Photo

*The hinny Amigo, donkey Jezebel's
offspring, was sired by Lori's stallion
Huckleberry.*

April 23, 1967
Helen Dengler Photo

Conspiracy or not, the outcome was "Amigo," a hinny, born April 23, 1967. The opposite of a mule, a hinny is smaller but just as sure footed, and was much favored by the pioneer women who trekked west with the covered wagons. Amigo's beautiful long ears, white muzzle and lustrous, long eyelashes, made him an instant favorite. Besides, he was wonderful to ride.

Until the 1950s and '60s, the Palm Springs desert area maintained its long tradition of riding in the "Wide Open Spaces." Horse trails had not yet reached the "endangered species" designation. Lori and her pals, wranglers Al Hein and Ed Burrus with our guests, could still ride at will down dry washes and up the canyons. On moonlight nights the sand dunes became a magical destination. Jack Boyer's Sunday morning Chuck Wagon Breakfasts featuring blueberry pancakes and cowboy singer Johnny Boyle, were a popular White Sun feature with guests, who could enjoy a horseback ride on the way.

Ian remembers an unusual method his father concocted for him to get to the Chuck Wagon Breakfast. Skis! Jack handcrafted a pair of metal skis he figured would glide over the sand, and planned to hitch them up to chubby little "Goldie," down at the corrals. When this novel approach to ski-joring failed, Jack was undaunted. With twelve-year-old Ian poised to charge off on the skis, he hitched him to the ranch truck! That too failed! Mercifully, ski-joring was abandoned!

Jack Boyer parked his chuck wagon under the tamarisk trees that lined Hank Gogerty's Desert Air landing strip. Children, perched above in the tree branches, commanded a bird's-eye-view of the breakfast crowd, where an occasional Hollywood star would be seated at the long tables below. Johnny Boyle knew them all.

"Say, I wonder if that little feller over there could be persuaded to put down his coffee cup for a minute, and sing a song with me?"

Johnny would move over, strumming the first chords of OH WHAT A BEAUTIFUL MORNING, as Gordon McRae put down his cup, to sing along. Johnny was always full of wisecracks, the next one aimed at Edgar Bergen,

With a bird's-eye-view of the performers below, the choice balcony seats go to children in the tamarisk trees, at Jack Boyer's Chuck Wagon Breakfast.

November 1956
Helen Dengler Photo

Edgar Bergen's ventriloquist act delights the breakfast crowd, which includes Palm Springs' mayor Frank Bogart sitting next to Boyer's wife, Keta (white hat).

January 1952
Photo courtesy Jack Boyer

141

Wrangler Ed Burrus sings "The Strawberry Roan" with Helen, during a steak-fry in the Kiva.

October 1962
Paul Pospesil Photo

The Strawberry Roan

*"His legs is all spavined. He has pigeon toes,
Two little pig eyes and a big Roman nose.
Little pin ears that touched at the tip,
And a big 44 run on his left hip.
He's ewe-necked and old, with a long lower jaw,
I could see with one eye he's a reg'lar outlaw."*

a frequent visitor, who was already shaping a female mouth on one hand with a borrowed lipstick. Draping a handkerchief over his knuckle for a bonnet, he would proceed with one of his famous ventriloquist acts.

If I had my accordion handy, Johnny insisted I join him with THE WANDERER, our ranch theme song, or he'd signal his beautiful Hawaiian wife, Tani, to close with an entrancing Polynesian song. Tani's coloratura soprano blended flawlessly with his rich baritone.

Sometimes wranglers are musicians. Ed Burrus' specialty was THE STRAWBERRY ROAN. He sang it with great fervor and eloquence, but never stayed in one key, making it hard to follow him with my accordion. Bob Spencer's SMOKE, SMOKE, SMOKE THAT CIGARETTE always stayed comfortably in one key. Nancy Carruthers was too bashful to sing, preferring to just play her accordion.

The five McCorkle boys worshipped wrangler Al Hein. They would follow him into the dining room for Al's coffee break, cowboy hats cocked at the same angle as Al's, the same chawing on a toothpick. Very solemn and respectful they sat with Al and their dad, Dr. McCorkle, faithfully imitating Al's every gesture down to the way he held his coffee cup. The doctor never so much as batted an eye when his youngsters had their cups filled with coffee! When I looked surprised, the doctor commented, "This is White Sun. We're all on vacation!"

I was soon to discover, "Pride goeth before a fall." On the day Al asked me to take out the riders on his day off, my heart swelled with pride. My string of eleven riders made the loop out to the sand dunes without incident, even dismounting to take pictures. On our return, within sight of the stables, Black Hawk suddenly shied at some imaginary obstacle, throwing me off. Somehow I clung to the reins and managed to walk him back to the corrals with some semblance of dignity. My string of riders followed in silence.

On another day, dismounting after a most invigorating gallop, and feeling very gay and silly, one of the girls mounted a horse, bareback. Following

Before they were paved over, desert storm drain channels made ideal riding trails.

November 1953
Helen Dengler Photo

her in a moment of abandon, I jumped up behind. That was one too much for the horse. Throwing me off, he rolled over me, a ton of cement, squeezing all the air out of my lungs. I was sure at least several ribs were broken. I tried hard to squeak, "I'm OK," but no words came out. At the doctor's office, I anticipated the worst.

"You're going to be sore for a while, Helen, but you don't have any broken ribs!"

Surprise! Even a little disappointment. They sure felt broken! But the doctor was right. It would take time and plenty of it to get over that soreness!

At a SITA Reunion Helen leads off with the rousing South African song, "Marching to Pretoria."

Venuto's Italian Restaurant, San Francisco
December 15, 1953
Moulin Studios Photo

146

chapter 10

Music Round-Up

Then the travel agency took Jack afar
He was always in Pretoria or Zanzibar
Leaving Helen / without a man
And all she had to squeeze was her "accordian."
She squeezed and she squeezed and she said, "Thank God"
That Papa sent me study-ing to Juil-li-ard.

Lyrics by Lloyd and Priscilla Dunn[1]
(Sung to the tune of The Admiral's Song by Gilbert & Sullivan)

Classical music held top priority over everything else when I was growing up in the Dykema family. Radio was still in its infancy and television had not yet arrived. The comedy team of "Amos and Andy," and the Nightly News, were the only radio programs my music professor Dad would tolerate. If they interfered with any of the five Dykema children's practice time, the radio was turned off. The only mechanical music we heard came from a wind-up Victrola, "His Master's Voice," playing those thick, 78 RPM records.

Jack went through a series of piano and violin lessons as a child, but he much preferred playing his guitar or the banjo. His special favorites were "The Little Red Schoolhouse," "Yes, We Have No Bananas," and "The Eddystone Light." At Hamilton College he formed his own band, "The Commodores," with visions of touring with them to Mexico. Little did he know that thousands of SITA travelers would be touring with him all over the globe, instead. On those early SITA bicycle tours, however, he did carry a guitar over his shoulder. Inevitably, it was music that first drew us together. Jack's voice singing those lively German folk tunes, was irresistible.

Lissa embarks on her musical career at age two, playing Helen's Steinway piano.

March 1956
Helen Dengler Photos

Gather round for "Home on the Range" at the weenie roast. Encircled by Mark, the Greenleafs, Ann Buccino, Helen, Nancy and Bella Bella, the dachsy, an ingenious ranch guest holds a plastic "heat shield."

November 1953
Lee Wenzlick Photo

In the Round-Up bar, the environmentally-friendly inventor Ed Burton sings his classic "Frozen Logger" song.

February 1959
Helen Dengler Photo

The Frozen Logger

As I sat down one evening, in a small cafe
A 40-year-old waitress, to me these words did say,
"I see that you are a logger, and not just a common bum,
For nobody but a logger stirs his coffee with his thumb."

150

Before I could truly adjust to desert living, White Sun needed a piano. We moved my beloved Steinway to the upstairs children's apartment, my Scandalli accordion, Jack's antique mother-of-pearl banjo, his Martin guitar and his ukelele. David's violin, Nancy's viola and Ian's flute came later. In the bar we installed an upright piano along with a full set of traps, not to mention a few eclectic relics that were hardly playable, but lots of fun for amateur tinkerers. We hauled our impressive Hammond organ up the stairs to the open loft above the lobby and added another grand piano to the Redwood Conference Room. Next, we found a piano teacher for the Dengler six, to carry on the Dykema tradition of piano instruction.

Our music backgrounds proved invaluable on SITA tours, and equally so at the ranch. Jack and I performed for outdoor steak fries in the Kiva, a recessed pit with a bonfire in the center, surrounded by long tables and benches. That was the place to go for Jean Schaffer's luscious, barbecued New York steaks and homemade apple pie. Birthday parties called for the accordion. There were memorable jam sessions in the bar with Jan Rouse (she took to percussion like a duck to water!), and talented guests, eager to join in. Ed Burton[2] could do marvels with the one-stringed guitar that hung on the bar wall, singing his unique lumberjack songs, such as THE FROZEN LOGGER. My accordion rode along on the New Year's Eve hay-wagon rides, climaxed with a children's Piñata Party in the lobby. Paul Bennett was always there to swing the guiding rope.

Ian maintains his music education came, not from the piano, but from the big White Sun loudspeaker, installed under the ranch windmill in the tower, audible even to distant neighbors. The controls were in the office where we kept our collection of LP records: movie and Broadway show tunes, Harry Belafonte, Perry Como, Olé Catarina, Odetta, Laurindo Almeida, Antonio Carlos Jobim, and folk music of all kinds.

★ ★ ★

We produced SONGS OF THE WHITE SUN in 1953, a half-hour LP record, featuring Johnny and Tani Boyle, with Helen and her accordion on the flip side. This major accomplishment came about with Jan Rouse's guiding hand and a lot of persistence. Johnny insisted the only way he would consider participating in a recording was to endure one taping session, only.

151

Let the stars, Nat King Cole or Crosby stand in front of a mike, taping the same song over and over to eliminate the tiniest flaw in the recording. He, Johnny Boyle and his wife Tani would sing each song flawlessly, the first time around!

Recording day arrived. Jan drove the four of us to Hollywood where we immediately set to work. Johnny tuned his guitar, beginning with WHO SHOT THE HOLE IN MY SOMBRERO? and continued without a break to his final duet with Tani. After the last note she involuntarily heaved a great sigh of relief.

Johnny threw a fit. He was sure she had ruined everything, and they would have to record all over again. He stomped out of the building to pace the streets. Allowing him plenty of time to cool off, I went ahead with my songs, closing with THE WANDERER, sung as a duet with Jan. When Johnny finally returned, he was informed that no further taping was necessary! Tani's sigh of relief had been easily erased.

This tall Irish cowboy Johnny Boyle, one-time beachcomber, chef, rope artist and musician, had been raised on the Bixby Ranch in California. There he absorbed the folklore, music, language and broad humor of the western cowboy and Mexican ranch hand that made him a favorite of presidents, millionaires, Hollywood stars and countless fans.

During the depression era Johnny found his way to the magic island of Tahiti, and its treasure-trove of Polynesian songs and dances. Small wonder he fell for, and married dark-haired, sloe-eyed, diminutive, Hawaiian-born Tani, the quintessential island beauty. Her silvery soprano blended so perfectly with his robust baritone. We felt doubly privileged when they performed at our weekly steak-fries and Sunday morning chuck wagon breakfasts.

The Palm Desert Chamber of Commerce invited Johnny to host a special Chuck Wagon Brunch to honor Konrad Adenauer, West Germany's extraordinary Chancellor. Adenauer and his party were on a whirlwind visit to the U.S. and were coming to the desert for two busy days of planned rest and recreation. Johnny, who spoke and sang Tahitian, but not German, thought

Campfires in the sand give way to steak fries in the Kiva, with Johnny Boyle singing his popular cowboy songs.

November 1963
Anonymous Photo

153

it would be appropriate to include some German folksongs in the program, so he called me. Would I come along to the brunch with my accordian, and sing? Folk songs have always been my favorites, German folk songs in particular. Of course I said yes.

It was a beautiful Sunday, March 20, 1960. The chuck wagon and tables were set outdoors in a scenic spot above Palm Desert, where THE LIVING DESERT now flourishes. The crowd was impressive, overflowing with statesmen, local dignitaries, and the press. I brought my Scandalli, and I sang. The Chancellor was delighted!

Capitol Records' Vice President, Lloyd Dunn and his wife Priscilla, along with a number of his business cohorts and friends, were frequent ranch guests. Lloyd happened to be an accomplished banjo player. One night, while jamming in the bar with some of his fellow musicians, he turned to me with a question.

"Helen can you play the 'PASSION SONG FROM LUCRETIA' on your accordion?"

Lloyd was known for his wit as well as his poetry, and I suspected this was a leading question. There are a number of "Lucretia" operas, but I couldn't identify this one.

"May I borrow your accordion?"

He picked it up, pressing the air intake button, and squeezed the bellows hard. No question about the resulting gasping and panting sounding undeniably like "passion," but most certainly not like any operatic aria!

The circular Capitol Records building, completed in 1960, became a familiar Hollywood landmark because of its shape, resembling a giant stack of records. The top floor conference room had been designed with state-of-the-art electronics. I was mystified when Lloyd phoned me one day to book a conference at White Sun.

"What's wrong with your conference room, Lloyd?"

"Oh, you can't be creative with all the sightseers and interruptions, and besides, we come up with much better ideas here in the desert, out riding or playing shuffleboard. You'd be surprised how creative we get at White Sun!" One of those better ideas was DUNN'S DIXIELAND DROPOUTS, a band of real pros, who performed three years in a row at the ranch.

White Sun proved a magnet not only for popular musicians, but classical as well. During Phil and Virginia Kraft's tenure in the 1950s, Kurt Herbert Adler, the innovative director of the San Francisco Opera, discovered the ranch. He would take a break after completing his touring season in Los Angeles, to bring his wife, Diantha (he called her "Bill"), and some of his opera stars and symphony players for White Sun quality time. In 1958 he invited me to come in to Los Angeles for the final performance of THE MARRIAGE OF FIGARO, featuring the Mozart diva, Elisabeth Schwarzkopf. She brought down the curtain to thunderous applause.

Kurt insisted, "After the performance, Helen, come along backstage to Elisabeth's dressing room, and then we'll go to the Brown Derby for supper."

Backstage at the theatre I was treated to another performance, a regular "mini-opera!" The cast members were all running around in various stages of undress, saying goodbye. You might think they were never going to see each other again! Wading through all the passionate embraces with considerable difficulty, I managed to find Elisabeth in her dressing room. She greeted me with her beautific smile.

"Kurt told me about you, Helen. Won't you please have a chair?"

As I waited, she put on tennis shoes and a trench coat. Her idea of "ranch attire" made me feel totally out-of-place in my high heels and finery. The ranch staff insisted I dress properly for "grand opera," so I was decked out in borrowed pearls, a mink stole and white gloves!

We drove out to Hollywood's Brown Derby for dinner. Elisabeth ordered poached eggs on toast, someone else wanted just salad and no dressing, a third, cereal. Everyone ordered something different. I just wanted to hit the road.

Nancy perches on the fences, with
Diantha and Kurt Adler, San Francisco
Opera director, to watch George
Boehme peddle by on his unicycle.
No hands!

December 1962
Helen Dengler Photo

156

Elisabeth Schwarzkopf
11 Nov. 58

Opera star Elisabeth Schwarzkopf (Mrs. Walter Legge) discovers White Sun, following her dazzling Los Angeles performance in Maestro Kurt Adler's MARRIAGE OF FIGARO.

November 11, 1958
Helen Dengler Photo

157

Back at White Sun the next day, Elisabeth welcomed an opportunity for a little gymnastic in the desert sunshine. She helped herself to a bike in the ranch bicycle corral and rode away to enjoy the rare thrill of exploring desert back-roads, completely unsupervised! She wound up at Ed Mullins' drug store in Palm Desert, shopped around the aisles and then strolled up to Ed's counter.

"Oh, I'm so sorry," she apologized, "I didn't bring along a purse!" Ed offered her a blank check, and helped her fill it out. Signing her name with a flourish, he was rewarded with another one of those melting smiles. For Elisabeth to have scaled the dizzy heights of an opera career, one that had taken years of dedicated and intensive training, heaven forbid that she should waste time with mundane financial matters! Money matters were her manager's problem.

Stepping out into the sunshine with her shopping bag slung over the handlebars, Elisabeth pedaled happily back to the ranch. Now she was quite ready for a swim, but alas, she hadn't brought along a bathing suit! She improvised, wrapping a diaphanous scarf around her hips, and another around her chest. After a refreshing workout in the pool, Elisabeth climbed out to execute a flawless headstand, poolside!

Some weeks later Ed Mullins phoned me. "Sorry to bother you Helen, but Elisabeth Schwarzkopf's check bounced." I assured him I would take care of the matter with her manager. No problem.

Kurt Adler took his gymnastic on the tennis courts, with frequent phone interruptions from overwrought prima donnas. He would patiently listen, soothing them in their native languages, providing clever solutions to their dilemmas, and then return to his game!

One day the desert experienced one of those infrequent cloudbursts that drench everything. Jack had been working on the roof over our second floor bedroom. Leaks were developing all over the ceiling and I was frantic, trying to catch them with an odd assortment of pots. I corralled Jack for help, when all of a sudden there was a loud knocking. I opened the door, and there in the pouring rain stood Kurt Adler. At that very moment, Jack grabbed a broom jamming its handle hard into the middle of the ceiling. A truly impressive flood of rainwater cascaded through the hole into a large bucket.

Whatever question was on Kurt's mind went begging. He turned away, muttering, "Effrey day I lurrn some-ting new!"

On another ranch visit Kurt brought along violinist Mafalda Gueraldi ("Muffy" Hooper), oboist Merrill Remington, and his cellist wife, Aurora, all seasoned professionals. They decided it would be fun to have a little evening chamber music, "Eine Kleine Nachtmusik," outdoors faraway from city lights. They chose nearby La Quinta Canyon for the setting, assuring me the glittering stars and a crescent moon would be sufficient lighting. They all knew the music by heart. That was the beginning of several delightful desert concerts, with unseen coyotes in the hills howling for encores!

Several years later when beehive hairdoes were in style, violinist Muffy survived an automobile crash that catapulted her through the car windshield. The glass splintered in her beehive hairdo, but Muffy was unscathed!

What should appear next tumbling out of a big bus one afternoon, but twenty-two Vienna Choir Boys with their director, Gerhard Lang. During their concert tour through Canada and the West Coast, these angelic-looking boy sopranos had been promised a swim in the White Sun pool. They made the most of their moment of freedom, boisterous German shouts and epithets ringing out in the desert air, taking me back to my school days at the Odenwaldschule. That evening they regrouped on the rustic lobby staircase, to serenade us with some heavenly music, closing with "Goode Nayet Laydeez, Weerr Goweng To Leeve You Now!"

Miss Angela Diller's arrival at White Sun came as a most unexpected and wonderful surprise. I had been a student at her remarkable Diller-Quaile School of Music for eight years, during my pre-college days in New York. Miss Diller and her colleague Elizabeth Quaile founded the school in 1921, and it's still going strong. The Diller Quaile School's rigorous standards of

The ranch pool provides some well-earned fun for the Vienna Choir Boys during their U.S. West Coast and Canada concert tour.

March 5, 1959
Helen Dengler Photo

musicianship were not for everyone. Miss Diller began reading music when she was three years old. "Before that," she said, "I played by ear!" She started teaching when she was twelve. Her teacher at Columbia University in New York, was the composer, Edward McDowell.

Every Saturday morning, while my friends were enjoying outdoor free time playing games, I commuted by train from Hastings-on-Hudson to New York City. My hands turned ice cold nervously anticipating arrival at the Diller-Quaile School. Formidable standards of musicianship and keen competition left no room for the timid. Before entering my keyboard harmony class I was routinely sent off to the bathroom to soak my hands in hot water.

Quoting from Miss Diller's KEYBOARD HARMONY COURSE, Book I, published by G. Schirmer, Inc. in 1936:

> Music is a language, just as French and Spanish and German are languages. In order to fully understand a French play when you hear or read it, you must learn to speak French; and, equally, in order to understand Music when you hear or read it, you must "speak" Music. The way to learn to speak it is by making your own music, as well as by reading music that other people have written.

Miss Diller attracted the best and the brightest in New York, and the competition was fierce and highly stimulating. She never stooped to our level, but always tried to raise us to hers. Although my technical skills on the piano never matched those of my fellow students, I found it easy to "speak" music, by making up my own compositions.

We began the harmony class with theory, ear-training and keyboard improvisation. (A private piano lesson always followed this intensive class.) Four pianos were lined up in front of us. Miss Diller would pick up a piece of chalk and write the basic chord structure, at random, on the blackboard for our improvisation, such as I-IV-V7-I (which happens to be the same opening harmonic structure as Bach's Prelude in C Minor).

Next she would choose a student for each piano, the first to improvise bass chords indicated on the blackboard simply as chords. The second player went further, breaking down those chords into arpeggios or some other variation. The third pianist improvised a melody, always in harmony

161

with the basic chords, and the fourth player could indulge his creativity by improvising a free-flowing, fancy obligato. With all four playing together it was impressive! We performed in any key Miss Diller requested. The entire process was unrehearsed, spontaneous, and never twice the same.

The program for the school's annual spring concert given at New York's Town Hall, included one of these four-piano improvisations. New York critics maintained we had worked on our improvisations for months. Well of course we had practiced many different chord examples for weeks, but never the ones Miss Diller dreamed up for the concert. That was always a challenge and a surprise. I was born with "relative pitch" and could usually anticipate where the harmony was leading. Improvising is a game I have always enjoyed.

Miss Diller (we wouldn't dare call her Angela), was still teaching piano students in her nineties! If we sat slumped forward, she would unceremoniously put a book on our heads to make us sit up straight. I was mortified when this happened to me once during a luncheon she hostessed. When she held recitals at the school, she would ask us all to stand, periodically, while she opened the windows wide on the chilliest New York winter mornings, and take a deep breath of fresh air.

Miss Diller was still going strong on that visit to White Sun, late in her life. Ernie Boyum, a regular at the ranch and a music lover who was always after me to sing Brahms Lieder, asked Miss Diller if she might give her a piano lesson (a first for Ernie). Of course Miss Diller did just that, the two of them having a wonderful time.

★ ★ ★

Christmas was the musical climax of every year for my Dad. His college students began preparing for the Christmas caroling season at the beginning of the fall semester. Starting several weeks before the holidays, the halls and campus of Teachers College at Columbia University rang out with all kinds of Christmas music.

Whether our family lived in the deep snows of Madison, Wisconsin, or Hastings-on-Hudson, New York, Christmas Eve was sacrosanct for caroling at neighbors' doors. With utmost stealth we would line up in front of

A Dykema/Dengler tradition brings the family together for Christmas Eve carolling around the neighborhood: David, Lori, Ian, Helen, Nancy's husband Al Goldschmidt, Nancy, Mark and Lissa.

December 24, 1960
Lee Wenzlick Photo

a house and break the frosty silence with HARK THE HAROLD ANGELS SING. In the old days there was no distracting interference from radios or TVs, and Christmas revelers inside the house could actually hear us. Front doors would open wide to reveal smiling faces and glimpses of bewitching Christmas trees. Dad always turned down the offers to please come in for refreshments, explaining we had to sing our carols at many more homes.

An event of great promise took place in the fall of 1962, within walking distance of the ranch. COLLEGE OF THE DESERT opened, the area's first junior college. Dr. John L. Norman, an outstanding choral conductor, headed COD's Music Department. It wasn't long before Dr. Norman became our good friend as well as Lissa's piano teacher. We invited him to bring his choir to the ranch for a Christmas Tea and to sing some Christmas carols. This proved such a success it became an annual holiday tradition.

It took a while to know desert neighbors, but by the time Lissa was four we were ready to perform our Christmas Eve caroling ritual around Rancho Mirage. Ranch guests were always invited to join the chorus with our family. Sometimes we had as many as five or six cars loaded with carolers.

Palm Desert friends had begged us to carol at their house, so off we drove, parking by their driveway, our candles at the ready. Unfortunately the family was having Christmas Eve dinner elsewhere. We found only the caretaker at home and he was about to dump two large, fully packed trash bags. Faced with the spectacle of a large chorus of carolers serenading him with lighted candles, should he empty the bags or should he hold them? Either solution seemed disrespectful. He held them. We sang our hearts out for him.

On our last call, we stopped at the Rancho Mirage postmaster's house, to sing for our good friends Sid and Laura Greenleaf. Apparently they had never experienced Christmas carolers before. As we raised our voices his front door opened a crack and a gun barrel poked out!

Poor Sid! Mortified with embarrassment he hastened to wish us "MERRY CHRISTMAS, and please, please, won't you all come in?"

White Sun's and SITA's West Coast Publicity Director Jan Rouse enjoys a happy hour with friends beside the pool.

1954
Yul Brynner Photo

chapter 11

Jan Rouse

From the start, word-of-mouth recommendations from enthusiastic guests began building an impressive guest list for White Sun. But Jack's ambitious plans to expand and improve the ranch facilities needed something more, an equally ambitious and creative promotional director. No qualified, dynamic individual fit that description better than twenty-four-year-old Janet Farrington Rouse of Pasadena, California, a 1949 SITA bicycle tour member.

Jan first heard about SITA from Art Dayton, also of Pasadena, whose children, Topsy and Bruce were members of my 1949 E-12A European Bicycle Tour. Art became an enthusiastic SITA tour organizer, influential in persuading Pasadena families to send their children on SITA tours.

An alumna of Pasadena's distinguished Westridge School for Girls, the University of California at Berkeley, and Stanford's Graduate School of Communications, Jan's multi-faceted talents as photographer, cartoonist, musician, writer, and public relations dynamo, as well as her vocation as a landscape architect, all qualified her as a natural for the White Sun/SITA team.

This symbiotic relationship of SITA with White Sun was a stroke of genius on Jack's part. World War II forced him to change gears. He not only needed to recreate his travel business, he needed a new approach, White Sun Guest Ranch! White Sun offered many possibilities: employment to young SITA tour leaders and tour members; a delightful setting for conferences, complimentary travel agent weekends, as well as a good

167

place to cement public relations with foreign dignitaries. When Jack established his SITA Headquarters at the ranch, it became the ideal training ground for overseas managers and personnel. Physical work on the ranch was another large bonus for Jack, as it satisfied his life-long passion for hands-on building and construction.

He was looking for someone to do a landscape job at the ranch, when he found Jan Rouse working on a similar job at a nearby Palm Springs hotel. Favorably impressed, Jack asked her to do some landscaping at White Sun. That was just the beginning. The next year he hired Jan as White Sun and SITA's West Coast Publicity Director, working out of SITA's Los Angeles office under manager Savi Latham. Before long, Jan's artistic talents blossomed into whimsical cartoons that enlivened the ranch newsletter, WHITE SUN ROUND-UP.*

On her weekends at the ranch, Jan enjoyed the Sunday Chuck Wagon Breakfasts, where Johnny Boyle held us all spellbound with his songs and quick wit. Why keep this talent hidden from the rest of the world, she reasoned. So she began a campaign to create a long-playing record, featuring Johnny Boyle with his guitar, and Helen Dengler with her accordion. There were hurdles to overcome, chiefly Johnny's stubborn resistance to the whole idea. He loathed cities. Any mention of a trip to a Hollywood recording studio just turned him off. Jan did not give up easily.

*All cartoons in this chapter by Jan F. Rouse.

Pasadena's Westridge School seniors take in the Sunday chuck wagon breakfast with balladeer Johnny Boyle.

November 4, 1956
Jan Rouse Photo

169

"She Wears Red Feathers and a Hooly Hooly Skirt," Johnny Boyle's *perennial favorite, includes singers Kathy Maclean, Jan, Helen and Lori.*

1954
Lee Wenzlick Photo

The success of that brainstorm resulted in the 1953 recording and Easter release of SONGS OF THE WHITE SUN, a 12-inch LP, made at Studio & Artists Recorders, at the intersection of Sunset and Gower, Hollywood's "Cowboy Gulch." The studio's chief executive, Lou Finston commented afterwards: "One of the best 'ranch-type' records I've ever had the pleasure of making!"

Jan's personal contacts proved invaluable in the Los Angeles area, especially her friendship with the L.A. TIMES Society Editor, Joan Burnham. Jan rarely missed an opportunity to spread the good word about White Sun and SITA. In 1953, on New Year's Day, she appeared on the Groucho Marx TV Show, promoting SITA's bicycle tours. Jan continues the story:

"I was a finalist on Groucho's Quiz show until Groucho asked me: 'How many black keys on a piano?' I knew there were 88 keys on a piano but the number of black keys [36] totally eluded me. My subsequent debate with Groucho over the trickiness of the question apparently was 'hilarious' ... and that show was picked as 'the best of Groucho,' and re-run on national TV four consecutive years! And for four years TV audiences also watched me trying to show Groucho how we changed gears on an English, 3-speed, Elswick SITA bike.

"Net result ... SITA's Bicycle Tours received thousands of dollars worth of free national publicity, sales ballooned, Jack was enchanted, and my friends called me 'Janet-36-Keys-Dumb-Rouse!' for those four years of re-runs."

Testing her out next as an assistant tour leader, Jack sent Jan off on a SITA Hawaiian-Study-Adventure-Schooner Trip, the summer of 1953. Her tour members came back with nothing but glowing praise. Then a more challenging assignment: SITA's first Foreign Scholarship Student Tour of the United States. Sponsored in part by the

Netherlands Government and SITA's Scholarship Fund, Jan, now the tour leader, had to deal with the idiosyncrasies of eighteen Belgian, Dutch, Italian and Swiss university students. They were in for one thrilling adventure!

Jan went out of her way to broaden the itinerary for them, VIP interviews in cities across the country, visits to friends' dude ranches throughout Arizona, topping it off with a visit to a Hollywood movie set, with Marilyn Monroe in person! This coup de célèbre was finessed with assistance from White Sunner, Dotty Neumann, herself a Hollywood star.

Jan fitted in more excitement for the group in Los Angeles: a visit to CBS-TV City to watch a Red Skelton rehearsal; a Hollywood Bowl concert; a ride in a 1914 Cadillac; and visits to both USC and UCLA campuses.

In 1958, Jan circled the globe when she was assigned to conduct a SITA Around-the-World Tour!

Her busy brain was always dreaming up new promotional projects. In 1954, when the ranch closed for the summer, Jan orchestrated a most improbable weekend at Bill and Fran Paulson's Catalina Guest Ranch. Only Jan could have thought up this one! As a publicity stunt, she coordinated three unlikely groups, all crammed together on board famous cowboy singer Roy Rogers' yacht, cruising from Long Beach, to Santa Catalina Island, off the southern California coast.

First priority went to Rogers' daughter, celebrating her sixteenth birthday with a bunch of her sophisticated teenage friends. Second priority, a group of unsophisticated

SITA's first European Scholarship Tour of the United States arrives in New York harbor. Kneeling at left, Tink Hobijn from Holland, becomes a key SITA staff member in charge of the European Tour Department at the ranch.

August 19, 1954
Jan Rouse Photo

German students on their first trip to the U.S., most of them needing the services of a translator. Jan took care of that, securing an invitation for me since I was fluent in German. The invitation also included daughter Nancy, baby Lissa, and my White Sun assistant, Kathy Maclean. Last priority, an evening farewell party for the Paulsons (on loan to White Sun during my pregnancy and the February birth of Lissa) who were returning to operate their own guest ranch on the island.

Being Jan, she managed to persuade all of us to come along on this wild journey. We packed up the accordion, a piñata, diapers, etc. for three-month-old Lissa (whom I took below decks to nurse in the privacy of Rogers' cabin). Nancy had made the large seahorse piñata for the evening's festivities, symbolizing the blue and white emblem of Catalina Guest Ranch, and as a special tribute to Fran and Bill in recognition of the great job they had done as White Sun managers.

Roy Rogers, himself, dressed in his familiar western outfit, boots, hat, and string tie, boarded the yacht just behind Kathy Maclean. She was wearing shorts, and the sight of her bare legs inspired him on the spot, to make up this mortifying little ditty: "She has freckles on the backs of her knees ... but she's pretty!"

Perhaps to avoid the mob scene on board or just for the fun of it, Rogers stepped into a smaller boat towed from the yacht's stern, to ride the foaming wake in privacy!

None of this made much sense, especially since Rogers' personal publicity agent was attempting to mastermind the scenario, and making little headway. With an L.A. TIMES photographer on board, Jan engineered yet another public relations coup for SITA and White Sun, reported with a full-page spread in the paper's society section.

My accordion soon had everyone singing aboard the yacht, except the birthday girl and her teenage friends who kept to themselves. Baby Lissa slept through it all, blissfully unaware of celebrities and the machinations of publicity agents! Later that evening at Catalina Guest Ranch, Rogers rejoined us, singing a generous share of his well known cowboy songs.

Westridge School's senior class "Ditch Day" proved to be a big winner, more effective ammunition in Jan's promotional arsenal than the Catalina Island experience. Ditch Day, a popular tradition among high school seniors, meant traveling as a group to some fantastic rendezvous, remote from school and home, on a fall weekend. The seniors could choose either Friday or Monday, to make it a three-day extravaganza. Jan, a Westridge School alumna, convinced the school authorities to book Ditch Day at White Sun for seven, highly successful years!

On their first Ditch Day, the Westridge girls came spilling out of a bus at the ranch entrance, prepared for all eventualities, carrying instruments, tennis racquets, and an amazing assortment of accessories. The only thing that was missing? Boys, of course, to appreciate the pulchritude so lavishly displayed poolside and on the diving board!

Jan timed their takeover to coincide with Palm Springs' Western Week Parade, for me an entirely forgettable event after my initial participation. The Westridge girls felt otherwise. In high spirits they sorted themselves out on a large hay-wagon, loaded with a full set of traps, three accordions, bongo drums, guitars and ukuleles. Much applause greeted their wagon along the route, and they also captured a parade award!

After Westridge discovered White Sun, other schools were quick to follow. Anoakia School's seniors were next in line. Jan's camera followed all these activities, her eye-catching photographs appearing in full-page spreads in the L.A.TIMES, thanks to her good friend Joan Burnham.

Here they come, the fifth annual invasion of Westridge School seniors, loaded with talent, bongo drums and sundry paraphernalia.

November 1958
Jan Rouse Photo

A Danish family living in Pasadena was the catalyst for Jan's next challenge, the making of our 25 minute, 16 mm. color/sound film, "UNDER THE WHITE SUN." Clemens Toft had first brought his wife and mother to White Sun in 1953. A skilled photographer, Clemens (known professionally as Clemens of Copenhagen) fell in love with the ranch, where he had met Jan. She was so enthusiastic about his photography, she talked him into making the film. She wrote the script and narrated the voice-over commentary.

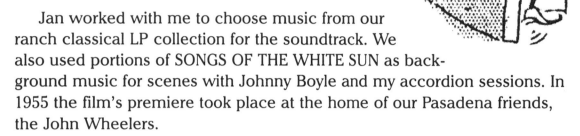

Jan worked with me to choose music from our ranch classical LP collection for the soundtrack. We also used portions of SONGS OF THE WHITE SUN as background music for scenes with Johnny Boyle and my accordion sessions. In 1955 the film's premiere took place at the home of our Pasadena friends, the John Wheelers.

Jan must also be given credit for bringing two bright, young Californians into the SITA/White Sun fold, namely, Kathy Maclean from Altadena, and Sue Hey from Los Angeles.

A childhood friend of Jan's, Kathy Maclean was a member of a two-month SITA European bicycle tour that Jan conducted in 1952. Once exposed to the magic of SITA, Kathy was off on a roller coaster ride! We often found leadership ability among the tour members, and Kathy was chosen to assist on a Western Camping Tour composed mostly of eastern teenagers, the summer of 1954. That same fall she became my White Sun assistant, acquiring the title, "Green Pea." Arthur Keleher taught her to play backgammon, and his affectionate name for her was "Kathy Pitty Pat" (the sound of her shoes scuffling over the flagstone patio).

"Green Pea" was hardly fair. Kathy was exceedingly bright, willing, attractive, and musically talented, although she tried to hide it all behind her spectacles. I was giving an accordion lesson one day in the lobby, when Kathy happened to be listening nearby in the kitchen. When the lesson was over, Kathy came out and picked up my accordion. Just by ear she had learned the song over which my student had been laboring, and she played it without a mistake!

I wasn't the only one besides Arthur Keleher who appreciated Kathy's finer points. Paul Ferguson, a guest at the ranch, recuperating from surgery, also discovered demure Kathy's charms, and fell in love with her.

Looking back at those golden fifties, it seems to me now that Kathy was a vital part of our ranch team for years. Actually she spent just one season at White Sun. Jack whisked her away to the SITA San Francisco office when the ranch closed for the summer, and that SITA job, too, lasted only six months. Paul Ferguson didn't want her out of his sight. He proposed marriage, and their wedding took place in December, 1955.

Paul and Kathy have lived happily in Las Vegas for the past forty-five years, raised two children, Peter and Paula, and delight now in their grandchildren.

Sue Hey arrived at White Sun in November, 1958. We had been looking for a SITA/White Sun assistant, when Jan Rouse told me she had found just the right person. Sue Hey was definitely the right person! Although Sue was not connected to Jan's Pasadena world, they had met through mutual friends of their parents.

After graduating from Stanford University, Sue spent six months traveling in Europe. Then she tried working in Los Angeles for two years with Paine, Webber, Jackson & Curtis, with another two years in central California's Tuolumne County. Not until then did she learn, through Jan, about our job opening at the ranch. Sue had no desire to work in a big city. She loved horses and what could be better than working at a dude ranch!

Sue started out in SITA's mailing and accounting departments, but was soon put in charge of the African and South American tour programs. In addition to her office work, since she was an experienced rider, she could spell Ed Burrus as a White Sun wrangler on his days off. During her last three years at White Sun, she kept her beautiful mare, "Bonnie," in the ranch corrals.

Round-Up Bar Hallowe'en quartet, Jan Rouse on traps, Kathy Maclean and masked Nancy Carruthers with their accordions and Helen at the piano.

October 31, 1954
Lee Wenzlick Photo

Sue Hey's favorite breed, Dalmatians Pepper and Jingo, fit right in with Tony Keroff's pinto ponies back in the corrals.

April 1968
Helen Dengler Photo

180

"We are Siamese, if you please!" Jan Rouse lines up five Denglers, Lissa, Nancy, Mark, Ian and Lori for a costume party.

May 1955
Helen Dengler Photo

181

Sue enjoyed life on the ranch as a versatile SITA employee until Jack sold his travel business to Diners Club. Eventually she chose Sonoita in southern Arizona, as an ideal retirement location, with plenty of riding space. Her comfortable adobe house is furnished with Western art, trophies from her foreign travels, a windmill that supplies water for the household, an assortment of cats, and her dog (a Dalmatian, of course). Everyone in Sonoita knows Sue, relying on her kindness and good cheer!

Jan Rouse is currently ghost writing a novel for an Hispanic author, following her long and successful career in travel, public relations, teaching marketing at UCLA, and working at Good Samaritan Hospital in Los Angeles. She is the author of the book, "I'M GLAD I'M ME."

Jan has always had an affinity with children. Just thirteen years older than our twins, Nancy remembers, "Jan was close to all of us, just like a big sister. We had no other relatives living anywhere near us, so she became ours, and was our beloved person."

Jan Rouse enjoys a sailing cruise with Vancouver, B. C. White Sunners, the Vern Kirkbys.[1]

August 1957
Photo courtesy Jan Rouse

White Sun's new manager, veteran hotelman Si Slocum, surveys the ranch with Helen.

October 1960
True Slocum Photo

184

chapter 12

The Slocum Era

"I'll work for free for the first month, to see if I like it, and to see if you like me!" Jack was interviewing Si Slocum for the job of White Sun manager. How could he turn that offer down? He didn't of course, and in the fall of 1960, Si was hired to do my job.

In the fifties, after Jack had worked so hard convincing me to become White Sun Manager and live at the ranch, it took him twice as long to realize he really wanted a private life with his family. His SITA Headquarters, now firmly established at the ranch was effectively operating an impressive network of overseas offices. SITA tours explored nearly every corner of the globe.

Jack felt this was the right time to move the Dengler family off the ranch to a home of our own on Old Prospector Trail, in Palm Desert. Nancy was married, David at the University of California, Berkeley, Ian at Stanford, and Mark almost ready for college.

The Slocum team, Si and his wife True, soon proved to be pure gold. With a lifetime of experience and talents we had yet to discover, our new managers never missed a beat stepping into my managerial shoes. Theirs was a marriage of both coasts, Si from Oregon, True from Massachusetts. Not only did they intuitively follow the established traditions of White Sun, they brought along a far-flung retinue of distinguished and devoted guests, who followed them everywhere.

Si Slocum, a Chi Psi business administration graduate of the University of Oregon, started off working with a travel agency, followed by twelve years of thorough training by hotelman, Leroy Linnard, at Santa Barbara's Samarkand and Pasadena's Vista del Arroyo Hotels. Horace Heidt found him at Soboba Hot Springs and prevailed on Si to come to the Lone Palm Hotel in Palm Springs, which he managed for eight years, with one year out as manager of Thunderbird Country Club. It took three more years, while Si managed Desert Skies and Casitas del Monte, before Jack found him.

True Greene Slocum might as well have come from another planet. She was born for the stage but luckily for us, it became the White Sun stage! She recalls her New England childhood when she pretended to be a robin, pressing her ear to the ground, listening for that big, fat worm. "I have always been fascinated by nature," she told me.

True met Si at the Vista del Arroyo Hotel in Pasadena, where she was applying for a job, after her Aunt Petie agreed to let her travel west with her on a cross-country drive from New York to California.

Before that, back in New York City, True had finished two years in business school, followed by a job at a Fifth Avenue jewelry store. On pay-days she was entrusted, unaccompanied, to carry funds to Wall Street amounting to thousands of dollars hidden in her padded coat. No Brinks truck for this intrepid nineteen-year-old!

In Los Angeles, after finding a room at the YWCA, True went out hunting for a job. She was advised to leave her name at Pasadena's Vista del Arroyo Hotel. The person in charge of hiring there was Si Slocum. She found him seated, with his feet up on a desk.

"What can you do?" he asked.

"I'm a touch-typist."

"We don't need anybody right now." End of interview.

Undaunted, True found herself a job with a Los Angeles jewelry store, with connections to her New York firm. A couple of days later Si phoned her at the YWCA for a date, and took her out dancing. A friend of Si's happened to be watching the dance floor and warned, "Watch out Si!"

Si watched out for all of four years. But after he was classified 4F by the Army, due to high blood pressure, the next time he bumped in to True at a bank he suggested, "I suppose June 14, 1941 is as good a time as any to get married?"

"Bird Lady" True Slocum earned her title from three-dimensional creations she fashioned with dessicated bits and pieces of wood collected in the desert. She calls them "Woodscapes."

April 1967
Helen Dengler Photo

187

True spent thirty hours putting her Roadrunner Woodscape together, made entirely out of ironwood in authentic roadrunner dimensions.

1969
True Slocum Photo

★ ★ ★

True's interest in art began early and she developed technical skills working in the jewelry business. Her unique "Woodscapes" took shape at White Sun. One of her greatest satisfactions in life was to see desert creatures, lizards, quail, roadrunners, spiders and snakes, take on life and motion from material which has no life at all. When people asked her, "With whom did you study?" she replied, "… under the greatest teacher of all, Mother Nature!"

It was Si who got True started on Woodscapes, when he offered her a piece of driftwood that looked for all the world like a rooster. She arranged him perched on a sand dune, against an orange sunrise, crowing, "What a great day this is going to be!"

During desert walks she took with her dog, Willie, True became adept at spotting some creature's likeness in the deadest bit of driftwood, greasewood, ironwood, juniper or, maybe just a plain palm frond. Under her experienced eye and skillful hands, that piece of driftwood became a three-dimensional picture, vibrant with life! Finishing them with colorful burlap backgrounds and a sprinkling of sand as a base, "Trusi's" Wood-scapes began to decorate guest rooms. No longer designated by number, a guest would request, "I would like the room with the quail!"

Martha Grether of Stockton, California encouraged True to hold her first one-woman show in Stockton, in May of 1966. Another one-woman show was quick to follow in Santa Fe, New Mexico.

"I had a place that I called my 'studio' in the breeze-way of my Rancho Mirage house," True explained to me. "I would work out there at times until 1 A.M., until I captured that third dimension and good stance. Then the next day or so I would do the labor [gluing, etc., holding it together]. Lizards were so curious. They would come and watch from their wall space for hours. They were my companions. I can't tell where it all came from—the love of the wood and the sense of joy, I think."

True's father had encouraged her to consider the theatre. She would have sparkled on the stage, but happily for White Sun, she showered her talents on the ranch. No telling what stunt she'd pull off on Hallowe'en.

189

In the ranch bar, sitting apart from the crowd, taking no part in the conversation, she disguised herself as "a Mysterious Stranger." Nobody figured out who she was.

Once the ranch season ended, the Slocums went camping in Montana for a complete change from torrid desert summers. They brought back glowing tales of Flathead Lake up in Montana's northwest corner near Glacier Park. I had never heard of Flathead Lake and wasn't much interested. Si kept dropping hints about Montana, until we finally decided to take a family vacation together, and see about this intriguing Flathead Lake. Jack trailered along his sailboat.

We found the Slocums camped on Flathead's west shore, in Big Arm State Park. There we joined Si, True and their son Emery, for two glorious weeks. Flathead Lake had water so clear you could drink it and see all the way to the bottom. Swimming was a bit chilly but exhilarating in such pure water, and the landscape was glorious.

It was a different Si who introduced us to fishing. With a sense of awe we watched his fly-fishing technique, something akin to ballet dancing! This Si was a far cry from the suave hotel manager, impeccably dressed, imperturbable in the face of crises. Si taught us to troll for Kokanee Salmon, where we could catch our limit almost any day and smoke them for a delicious treat to pack along on hikes into the Mission Mountains.

We explored Glacier Park together, hiking the beautiful Garden Wall Trail to Granite Park Chalet, and meeting bighorn sheep or ground-hugging marmots that would try to lick the salt-sweat off our shoes! One day we stepped over a warm cake of bear dung and soon afterwards spotted a grizzly. Fortunately he didn't spot us! When we reached the chalet, people thought Si was a botanist, since he could identify all the lovely Alpine wildflowers.

Back in Big Arm State Park, True would round up children, as many as a dozen at a time, like the Pied Piper of Hamelin, for a night's camp-out on the hill above the park. They would cart along their sleeping bags, but that was not all. Even watermelons! With True leading the way, they'd

During a summer vacation, Jack studies master fly fisherman Si Slocum, casting his line in the Thompson River.

Thompson Falls, Montana
July 1961
Helen Dengler Photo

191

cart along anything. Reaching the top they'd celebrate with a midnight feast. They christened the spot Watermelon Hill. True's charm and daredevilishness were simply irresistible.

The Slocums had a unique camping ritual. Before leaving wherever they camped, they would dig a small hole on the site, fill a glass jar with memories of their summer there, cap the jar and bury it in the hole. True remembers the last jar they buried on Wildhorse Island out in Flathead Lake. "I know the exact spot," she assured me.

Flathead Lake became such a favorite refuge we finally purchased a waterfront lot on Elmo Bay, where Jack built an A-Frame house cantilevered over the water. Never done building, the next project was the Red Barn for boat storage. In 1977, we converted it into a cozy, year-round home for family, *and* guests.

Because of the Slocums we fell in love with Montana and now, every spring and fall, we migrate along with the birds between Texas and Flathead Lake.

When we lost Si, in 1974, True became co-manager of White Sun with Kathy Williams, a former ranch guest. True eventually gave up her Woodscapes to become an inspired painter. She now lives with her second husband, Steve Taft, in Fallbrook, California.

Kathy Williams, who had met the Slocums first at Lone Palm Hotel in Palm Springs and followed them to Rancho Mirage, became White Sun's last manager, when True remarried. Kathy still lives in Palm Desert, devoting much of her time as a volunteer for The Living Desert.

192

Montana's Flathead Lake became my lifetime addiction due to this triumvirate: Big Arm State Park ranger and poet, Golden Bibee, and White Sun managers True and Si Slocum. Joining them amidst the lake's shoreline driftwood: Emery Slocum, his beagle Hattie, and the Dengler dachshund, Nikki.

August 1967
Helen Dengler Photo

Les bons vivants! Arthur Keleher confessed he was a pushover for a picnic and so, too were Clara de Lendrecie (under hat) with her jolly companions Charlie and Ann Hibbert, and Cousin Avelina Bowlin.

Hidden Valley, Joshua Tree National Monument
February 1963
Helen Dengler Photo

chapter 13

Clara de Lendrecie

C is for the crowds she draws around her
L is for the late hours she keeps
A is for the aristocratic lady
R is for the Royal Court she keeps
A is for the alcohol she buys us—
Even though she makes a great big fuss.
Put them all together, they spell CLARA,
A name that means White Sun, to us!

—Ginny Wertz

The White Sun guest most likely to vie for top honors with Arthur Keleher, has to be Clara de Lendrecie, "Queen of the Frozen Dakotas." She arrived at the ranch from Fargo, North Dakota, some eight years after Arthur's 1955 departure, and was greeted by True and Si Slocum. True remembers "… how Clara and her cousin, Avelina Bowlin walked in, and asked if they could stay for a long time."

"We're all filled up, ladies," Si replied, "… except for this week." Clara and Avelina checked in. That night in the bar Clara ordered a double martini.

Si Slocum changed his tune. He decided they could stay all winter, … and Clara did!

She must have been in her late eighties then, fighting her doctor's recommendation to quit smoking. She always carried a small, suede bag with cigarettes and a little scissors to snip each one in two, assuring her doctor she was quitting, by smoking only half!

A born aristocrat, impeccably dressed, and gracious, Clara charmed us all. But she was something of a shocker, too. When I made the rounds of the dining-room tables, to ask if anyone would like to join a picnic outing to Joshua Tree National Monument's Hidden Valley, Clara and Avelina were the first to raise their hands. I hesitated, explaining this would involve some rough going, crawling on hands and knees through a tunnel, under huge boulders. To prove her fitness, Avelina promptly did the splits right there on the floor! As for Clara, well, you just didn't say no to Clara. They both joined our expedition, crawling through the tunnel on all fours, and even walking up the great stony neck of the "Trojan Horse," as we had named it.

It seemed only right and proper that Clara would choose No. 22, Arthur Keleher's room, strategically located across the patio from the lobby entrance. Seated at her window with a green visor shielding her eyes from the brilliant desert light, Clara could watch everyone coming and going. This vigilance soon earned her the title, President of White Sun Guest Watchers' Society. In fact, newcomers often mistook Clara for the ranch owner!

When Easter came along, Clara became a spectator at Lori's Horse Shows, where she found a seat in the shade of the pepper trees. Saturday nights she took in the square dances out on the badminton court, where Harry Kester directed the "allemande lefts" and "do-si-dos" with his long, pointed finger. On sunny afternoons by the pool, she'd monitor Ernie Molloy and Fred Ingold, "The Montgomery Street Domino Champs," who sat together under a striped umbrella, concentrating on their game. Perhaps she'd prefer a commanding spot on the dining room terrace, with its sweeping view of the nine-hole pitch and putt golf course. By shifting her gaze to the wide open desert behind the ranch, she'd catch a glimpse of Ed Burrus and his string of riders disappearing over the sand dunes, or somewhere around the place there was Jack, stripped to the waist, hard at work mounted on his tractor.

I experienced a very poignant moment with Clara one afternoon at my Palm Desert home.

After crawling under boulders through the secret entrance to Hidden Valley, Clara found walking up the back of the "Trojan Horse" a lot easier.

Hidden Valley, Joshua Tree National Monument February 1963
Helen Dengler Photo

Afficionados Clara and Avelina chose a shady spot under the pepper trees to watch Lori's Easter Horse Show.

March 20, 1964
Helen Dengler Photo

198

None of my immediate Dykema family members had ever visited White Sun, except my youngest brother Peter Scot. In 1966 both my mother and Aunt Helen made their one and only visit, flying out from New York to Los Angeles, where I picked them up. There was so much I wanted to share with them, especially Clara de Lendrecie!

I invited Clara to meet these two Dunning sisters, my mother of five, grandmother of sixteen, Jessie Dunning Dykema, and spinster Aunt Helen, who had devoted years of her life helping mother raise her brood, and more years, later, helping me raise mine. A word about the Dunnings.

I had always stood in awe of Grandfather Ira Smith Dunning. As a teenager he traveled West with the covered wagons in the California Gold Rush, followed by service in the Civil War. Ira was a stern, forbidding presence, an avowed atheist and a civil engineer.

A devoted Catholic, Grandmother Katy Cargan Dunning was a teenage survivor of Ireland's terrible potato famine, who escaped to America. She found work as a serving girl in the Dunning's kitchen.

Following his gold mining adventures and the Civil War, Ira came home to marry Katy Cargan. On the farm he homesteaded in Iowa's Nishnabotna Valley, he personally delivered Katy's four daughters, one after another, Jessie being the youngest. She was a painfully shy girl, ill at ease with strangers, a homebody, completely devoted to her family. However, she inherited some of Ira's stubborn, adventurous spirit. Against her parents' wishes she married Peter Dykema, a Dutch Calvinist music educator. He firmly believed every human being was born with music. All it takes is the right environment to bring it out.

He proved his point, too, bringing out music in all the Dykema children, but not in Jessie, who resisted. She sang to us but held back on piano lessons. She didn't want to compete with us. Not until we were all grown up and gone did she finally begin piano lessons. Once or twice on visits to my Dykema home in Hastings-on-Hudson, New York, I had heard mother softly playing our old Mason & Hamlin grand.

After introducing Clara to mother and Aunt Helen, an amazing thing happened. Uninvited, Mother sat down at the piano and began to play for her! I was dumbfounded. Her arthritic fingers managed to find the right notes and skillfully performed Beethoven's Minuet in G, minus the variations. Clara was impressed, but not nearly as much as I!

Everyone confided in Clara, including the staff. She missed nothing. If some night owls found the Round-Up-Bar closed, they could depend on a beckoning light in Clara's window. In her room, she always kept a bureau drawer filled with bottles lying prone. Clara's bar was never closed.

Bartender Joe Noster remembered the night Clara felt a little unsteady on her feet. He offered to walk her to her room. "You know, Joe," she whispered, "I think I'm becoming a lush!" Si recalled another prize Clara comment, when it was time to drive her to the airport, for her flight back to Fargo. She was keeping him waiting longer than usual, and he asked if there was any problem.

"Sorry if I kept you waiting, Si, but I had to put on my bloomers, because if the plane crashes, I've got to be decent!"

After Clara could no longer travel, she retired to her favorite hotel in Fargo. She vowed she'd never under any circumstance, be trapped in a nursing home. In Fargo, Clara's husband had founded the department store, "de Lendrecie's," famed for its china department. When our eldest son, David, announced in 1973 he was getting married at a friend's home near Boston, I instantly thought of de Lendrecie's as the ideal place to shop for his present. As luck would have it, the wedding took place on Valentine's Day, when Fargo might as well have been the North Pole. But I couldn't miss this chance to see Clara again. I booked my flight to Boston via Fargo.

Emerging from the airport to find a taxi, the frigid air took my breath away, and I had to walk backwards into the wind. When I reached the hotel, Clara was waiting just inside the door, apologizing up and down for not greeting me at the airport. Her health was frail, but her spirit was indomitable. She steered me into the hotel dining room for a delicious meal, and a long catch-up on all the ranch gossip.

Two distinguished ladies meet in White Sun's patio, Major General Rapp Brush's widow Alice, and Clara de Lendrecie, "Queen of the Frozen Dakotas!"

March 1964
Helen Dengler Photo

201

*From her cabin No. 22 directly opposite
the main ranch entrance, Clara could
observe White Sun's passing parade.*

March 1970
Helen Dengler Photo

202

I finally got around to asking if she had any suggestions for David's wedding present? Of course she did. "Try out the china department, Helen, it was my husband's favorite."

I went alone to de Lendrecie's the next day. Clara had already assigned a young salesman to be my counselor, and I certainly needed counseling in that vast array of magnificent china! I took my time, lingering, torn over the choices, but finally chose a pattern I was sure the young bride would love. I gave Clara my detailed report over lunch. Some weeks later I learned she had insisted that my young salesman bring her samples of the china pattern I had chosen. Clara approved.

That was my last visit with Clara. She had her wish and never went anywhere near a nursing home.

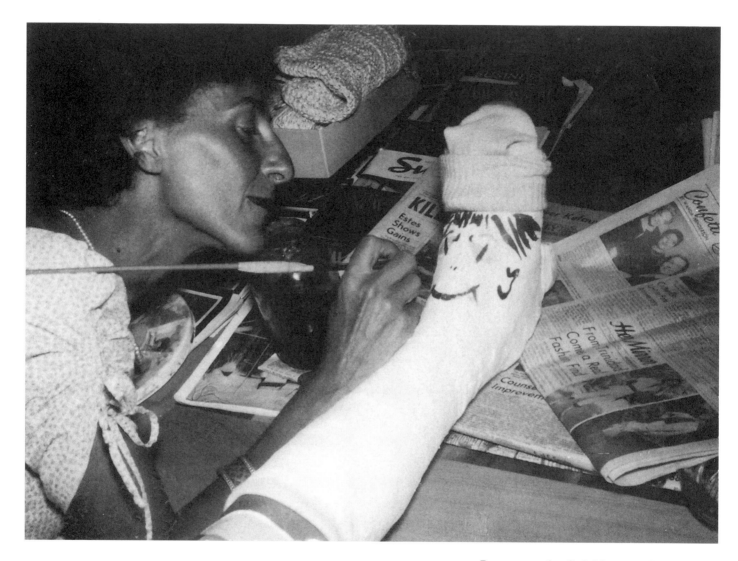

Dotty puts the finishing touches on "Dreamy Pete," Blanche Vanstrom's leg cast.

April 1956
Helen Dengler Photo

chapter 14

Dorothy Neumann

"Don't Never Shake My Persimmon Tree"

Dotty Neumann became an official member of the Dengler family when Lissa, our three-year-old, began calling her "Daddy Omens." I wasn't three but closer to ten, when I first met Dotty at the Neumann's apartment in New York City, way back in 1924. My father, Professor Peter W. Dykema, and Dotty's father, Dr. Henry Neumann, were good friends. Neumann was the distinguished leader of the Brooklyn Ethical Culture Society. They had met at New York City's Ethical Culture School when Dad taught music there, from 1901 to 1913.

All I remember of my first encounter with the Neumann family, during the chilly depths of a New York winter, were Dotty's bare legs, little white ankle socks and Mary Jane shoes. In the Dykema family, I wore long, lisle stockings well above my knees, held up by my BVD garters. No shiny patent leather Mary Janes on my feet, but sturdy, scuffed, brown leather boots, laced up well over the ankles. For me, Dotty's bare legs were a source of wonder, amazement and bravado.

When we moved from Madison to New York City, Dad enrolled the youngest Dykemas, Peter Scot, six, and Helen, ten, at the Ethical Culture School, his old stamping grounds on 64th Street, facing Central Park West. At Ethical, my legs were a source of wonder and amazement to my classmates. They swung me up on a table, curious, the better to view my underpinnings, my lisle stockings and my boots! This hayseed from the wilds of Wisconsin constituted a genuine novelty for these sophisticated New York kids.

As if that mortification were not enough, I was required to repeat fourth grade, which I had already completed at a one-room country school in Wisconsin. However, there was some compensation. During math class I was selected to paint scenery for an up-coming production of "Peter Pan." With my back to the class I happily wielded a paintbrush, while the rest of the children labored over their arithmetic.

Many years later, during the early forties when the Dengler family lived in Los Angeles, we had the good fortune to discover the Turnabout Theatre, a dual-stage cabaret and puppet theatre, already a Hollywood legend. Stars like Elsa Lanchester, Lotte Goslar, Frances Osborne, Odetta, Marais and Miranda, and Dorothy Neumann, regularly appeared on its live stage.

Turnabout was the creation of three gifted men, the Yale Puppeteers. Forman Brown wrote all the clever songs and sang them as he played the piano. Harry Burnett, marionette craftsman supreme, was the puppeteer. Roddy Brandon kept everything on track as business manager. The name, Turnabout, derived from the theatre's reconditioned trolley car seats. During the intermission that followed the marionette show at one end of the theatre, a conductor blew his whistle, announcing, "End of the line, folks. Flip your seats!" Around they would go, to face a live review stage at the opposite end of the theatre. A dummy audience sat in the balcony on one wall, oblivious to the announcement. It was repeated rather gruffly, at which point a switch automatically turned the elegantly clad puppets about.

Turnabout's witty, sophisticated, adult entertainment lasted until 1956, when the show finally closed its doors. By that time, in between her various movie roles, Dotty Neumann had become a regular guest at White Sun. Here was an actress devoid of affectation or Hollywood glamour, down-to-earth, a creative inspiration so compelling, our baby Lissa decided to become, not just an actress, but a star, like Dotty.

Whenever the ranch seethed with the ferment of a SITA Reunion, Dotty was there to help create props and scenery, whatever the production lacked. A virtuoso performer, at Steak-Fries or Breakfast Rides, we'd clamor to have her sing her trademark song, "Don't Never Shake My Persimmon Tree." "Tree" had been specially written for Dotty, by Forman Brown, for her solo comedy act at Turnabout. With a sly smile she'd softly begin:

When in need of a prop man just ask Dotty, busy decorating the Theresien Terrasse for SITA's Oktoberfest, assisted by Ruth Vesey, Pat Teller and Lissa.

October 13, 1962
Helen Dengler Photo

207

Don't Never Shake My Persimmon Tree

Go to sleep my chinkapin, don't you never peep
And mammy'll spin for you a tale to send you off to sleep:
There was a lady dark of brow, with heart of hardest stone
And high upon a mountain top this lady dwell't alone.
And when a lover come to woo, this purty song sang she:
If you don't like my persimmons, don't never shake my tree.
Don't never shake, don't never shake, don't never shake my tree.

A lover come from out the West, so handsome bold and spry.
She stuck a dagger in his breast, her finger in his eye.
And as she watched the blood gush out, this purty song sang she:
If you don't like my persimmons, don't never shake my tree.
Don't never shake, don't never shake, don't never shake my tree.

A lover come from out the East, with purse so full of gold.
She drawed a rope around his neck till he was blue and cold.
And as she watched his eyes pop out, this purty song sang she:
If you don't like my persimmons, don't never shake my tree.
Don't never shake, don't never shake, don't never shake my tree.

A lover come from out the South, before she'd time to act.
He grabbed an axe and in four chunks that cruel girl he whacked.
And as he flang each piece away they sang in harmony:
If you don't like my persimmons, don't never shake my tree.
Don't never shake, don't never shake, don't never shake my tree.

★ ★ ★

Generous to a fault, Dotty shared her friendship with Turnabout stars with us. She introduced me to South African balladeer, and composer, Josef Marais and his delightful wife, Miranda, who performed with him on stage and recordings. I had been eager to meet Marais because his "Wanderer's Song," with its graceful words and lovely melody, became SITA's theme song, and then, White Sun's.[1]

★ ★ ★

Odetta Holmes was born in Birmingham, Alabama in 1930. She was hoping to become an opera singer when she began to perform at Turnabout, while

208

still a teenager. But opera was not to claim her. Instead she became a dynamic force in American folk & blues music, still going strong in her 70s. In the late 1950s, Dotty brought Odetta to the ranch for a festive holiday concert. Seated in front of our ranch fireplace with the guitar she had named "Baby," wearing colorful Afro-American finery, she mesmerized everyone with her stunning deep voice. Though she had taken voice and piano lessons as a child, her guitar-playing is unique, self-taught, and has become known as "the Odetta strum." I love her rendition of the lullaby folksong, "All The Pretty Little Horses."

A favorite with the guests and my family, Dotty was inspiration and role model for Lissa. In 1973 she enrolled in Boston's Emerson Performing Arts School, but that lasted only a year. She complained, "They're all on an ego trip, Mom!" She transferred to Boston University to major, instead, in piano performance.

Dotty was always ready and willing to participate in whatever activity we were planning, maybe an excursion to collect dried up bits of desert plants for True Slocum's "Woodscapes." True transformed these bits and pieces, spending long hours carefully rearranging them to create Road-runners, Gambel's Quail, and other desert creatures. Any trip was more fun with Dotty! And what a thrill for Lissa when Dotty took the time to pre-view Lissa's and her buddy Christina McCandless' newest puppet show!

Dotty never took a SITA tour but she enjoyed being a part of SITA Reunions. We considered her a member of the family. The last time she joined us was on New Year's Day 1992, at Jack's 80th birthday party and SITA reunion at the YO Hilton, in Kerrville, Texas.

White Sun's immortals: Arthur, Clara, and Dotty.

Dotty and Nancy examine the flora in Joshua Tree National Monument.
1967
Helen Dengler Photo

Jean Schaffer, White Sun's incompara-
ble chef, was always full of surprises.

May 1962
Helen Dengler Photo

chapter 15

Kitchen Tales

Chefs come in all sizes and shapes and the ranch had its fair share. But nobody was in Jean Schaffer's class. She was a gift straight out of culinary heaven! Jean and her husband Mitch hailed from Allentown, Pennsylvania. Jean's parents came from Czechoslovakia, Mitch's parents from Germany. He had been an electric welder and president of his local United Steelworkers Union. He kept a bunch of rags stuffed in his hardhat in case strikebreakers hit him over the head. Jean worked in the needle trade, was a Red Cross and YWCA volunteer, lifeguard and swimming teacher. Later they ran a motel in Lake George, New York.

Because the Schaffers often organized winter outdoor activities for Batona (Back to Nature) and the American Youth Hostel Association, a friend suggested they get in touch with SITA. They were well qualified. When they phoned the New York SITA office they just happened to catch Jack, who arranged for an interview. It went so well he signed them up to conduct the Ranger Bicycle Tour, a camping trip in the West for teenagers. Jean had done lots of volunteer work with young people and both Schaffers proved highly effective as tour leaders.

I well remember watching the scene in New York's Grand Central Station at the conclusion of one of their SITA camping trips. Anxious parents were welcoming sons and daughters home, but the kids clung to Mitch and Jean with tears streaming down their faces, loath to let go.

After their second successful summer with SITA in 1952, we invited the Schaffers to White Sun, offering Mitch the job of groundskeeper, and Jean full charge of the kitchen. She remembers, "It was a new venture for me. At first I paced the floor, nights. What shall I serve the guests? Well, I couldn't serve the same food as on the Ranger Cycle Tour! I will try my best. Home cooking was put on the menu and I took off from there."

"Many hours were spent in the kitchen. One day Jack asked me, Jean, what do you do all day? Well, he wanted me to make a list of the employees and just what each person did. There were at least seven people to account for. So one day I found a pair of roller skates in the back room, and at lunch time I put them on. They made a racket on the floor. Jack looked into the kitchen to ask what was going on. Oh, I said. I'm behind in my work so I move a little faster if I use skates. Perhaps when I catch up I may get that report you asked for!"

While living in Allentown, Jean and Mitch enjoyed frequent weekends with friends and VIPs hiking in the nearby Pocono Mountains. On one such outing Jean added a picnic surprise. When the hikers reached the top of the mountain, far removed from roads or civilization, Jean announced:

"The Ice Cream Man is coming!"

She and Mitch disappeared behind some trees where they had cached their surprise. The previous week she had been packing ice cream into a wide-mouth thermos, adding a little every day and packing it down hard. She kept it in her freezer. Even after the four hours of climbing, the ice cream in the thermos remained solid.

The astonished hikers were offered cups of frozen ice cream!

Jean's sense of humor didn't change at the ranch. She had special surprises for birthdays, depending on the honoree's good sportsmanship. Look-alike-apple-pie for instance, using nylon stockings instead of apples! What a shock when the first piece was cut out! Another shocker, Jean's Cotton Birthday Cake, was a prize, beautifully frosted with fancy flowers and the birthday person's name, looking for all the world like the real thing!

All smiles, the honoree would protest, "Aw' you shouldn't have done it!"

He attempts to cut a slice. The frosting bounces up and down, the cotton refusing to give. The victim perseveres and becomes agitated. Reddening, he finally puts down the knife in defeat. At that moment the kitchen door opens and Jean enters with the real birthday cake, candles glowing!

(To create this surprise, buy a big roll of cotton, cut it in large rounds,

To visit Niagara Falls, everyone on Mitch and Jean Schaffer's teenage SITA tour is issued a poncho, on board the MAID OF THE MIST.

July 1952
Photo courtesy Jean Schaffer

stack them up like a layer cake and then decorate with real frosting and birthday candles. Do keep it a secret!)

Jean's training included hotel school but no formal cooking instruction. Her genius was intuitive. Year after year she turned out mouth-watering food, elegant sauces, and luscious desserts. Along with all her talent she maintained an elfin sense of humor.

I asked how she ever found time to sit down and eat?

"Well, Helen, I never did sit down but don't worry. I had my snack."

"And what was that, Jean?"

"A toasted rye bread sandwich with ice cream inside!"

It was uncomfortably hot in the kitchen before Jean Schaffer took over. There was no air conditioning at first other than "swamp coolers," noisy water evaporaters which were ineffective if humidity was in the air. David remembered an early summer working at White Sun, "… when temperatures were awful … We had to drive to Palm Springs for all our supplies, especially ice blocks for the ranch ice chest. We had no refrigerator at that time. Ice was always the last item on the list and it began promptly to melt in the heat."

David's kitchen job was to swat flies, which abounded in summer, with only a screen door to keep them out. So this enterprising ten-year-old left the screen door slightly ajar to augment his income. His remuneration was a penny per pile of 25 flies!

When I became ranch manager in 1951, the chef I inherited was an artist and very creative. She disdained leftovers, however. On one of her days off I investigated the condition of the kitchen refrigerators, (we did have refrigerators by then) and was appalled by the spoilage. I went to work dumping everything moldy or otherwise inedible, and scrubbed out the refrigerators. When the chef discovered my meddling the next day she was so insulted she yelled, "I'm quitting!" I was relieved to accept her resignation on the spot.

The family's relationships with guests were close and long lasting. Here's one of our favorites, "Mommy" Dot Nilon, celebrating her birthday with pals Lori and Mark. The real thing or one of Jean Schaffer's cotton birthday cakes?

1955
Helen Dengler Photo

Chow hounds Helen, Carolyn Sundin, Ted and Beryl Tilbury, and Eda Beronio stack their plates at the lunch buffet.

May 1956
Paul Pospesil Photo

218

For lunch al fresco, load your tray at Jean's bountiful buffet and carry it out to the patio.

November 1957
Helen Dengler Photo

I knew it would be my turn in the kitchen one day. When that day arrived I was determined to serve a special treat, my Aunt Helen's lemon meringue pie, always my favorite. Aunt Helen had shared her treasured recipe with me so I felt confident and ready to take over. Now it was my turn. I made the pie shells rolling out the dough on canvas just as she had taught me, and set them aside to finish the lemon filling. After pouring the filling into the raw pie shells I set them in the oven. Something told me to double-check the recipe. Horrors! I should have baked the pie shells first and then poured in the filling. Disaster!

That day the guests had to make do with plain old ice cream. Seems like everything ends up ice cream!

White Sun featured the American Plan. Just help yourself to big platters steaming on the table. The old ranch bell on the patio wall rang three times a day to summon the hungry guests, 8:30 breakfast, 12:30 lunch, and 6:30 dinner. You could tell the days of the week by Jean Schaffer's dinner meals.

Sunday:	Baked chicken with tangy Hungarian green beans, scalloped potatoes and creamy fruit salad
Monday:	Honey glazed ham with mustard or cherry sauce, potatoes, and green salad with garlic dressing
Tuesday:	Stuffed cabbage rolls with mashed potatoes, candied carrots, corn muffins and salad with creamy fresh basil dressing
Wednesday:	Roast leg of lamb with fresh mint sauce, mashed potatoes, green beans or beets with toasted walnuts and four-bean salad
Thursday:	Veal paprikash with spaetzle (drop noodles), hash brown potatoes, and Pennsylvania Dutch salad with bacon dressing
Friday:	Baked white fish with tartar or horseradish sauce,

	scalloped potatoes, sauced red beets and salad with cilantro vinaigrette
Saturday:	Outdoor steak fry, baked potatoes and sour cream, fresh garlic buttered sourdough bread, green salad and home-made apple pie

★ ★ ★

Playing multiple roles is an essential part of guest ranching. As White Sun manager it was a courtesy and my pleasure to be seated with the guests first thing in the morning. Most of them had become good friends by then. But when unavoidable I had to excuse myself and dash off as a substitute for a sick maid, help out in the kitchen, or replace some other no-show. No telling where or when the next emergency might occur.

It occurred in a wall heater. Who else but an Army Major General would sound the alarm! On a chilly Monday morning in January 1956, Major General Rapp and Alice Brush discovered a wall heater shooting a long tongue of flame into their room. Suddenly, flaming pilot lights were out of control all over the ranch. Our butane gas tank filter had broken down, undiluted gas flowing directly into all the lines.

General Brush marshaled his forces, guests and staff alike, and we leapt into action. His troops cut off the gas lines and we conquered the flames! The kitchen was spared, the ranch was spared. Only one bedroom unit sustained considerable damage. That was White Sun's first trial by fire but not the last. A greater test of the ranch's resilience loomed fifteen years ahead.

On the eve of Thanksgiving at 10:49 P.M., on November 23, 1971, our next-door neighbors Mike and Ann Buccino were just turning in for the night. Ann noticed flickering lights in the ranch tower.

"Look Mike! White Sun must be celebrating a special party!"

"Oh no, Ann, I don't think so. We better call the fire department!" Mike grabbed the phone.

This time another wall heater in the tower bedroom was the culprit. Bedding had been pushed too close. Departing guests left the heater on and

221

didn't notice. Jack's New Zealand paintings and our entire collection of vintage guest scrapbooks happened to be stored in the tower. Somehow all survived the fire with only serious smoke damage, and were cleaned, restored, and useable!

It took thirty-four volunteer firemen working a total of 120 man-hours, to bring the tower fire under control. Water damage to the kitchen and dining room directly below, was extensive and the total bill ran over $75,000. Two of the firemen sustained lacerations to their hands, while battling the blaze and were taken to the hospital for stitches, and then released. Somehow Jean Schaffer managed to prepare a feast for the firemen, even though Thanksgiving was the very next day!

Like other major holidays, Thanksgiving was always packed to overflowing. Many of our guests were already on their way to the ranch and it was too late to cancel reservations. Mop-up crews were still in the kitchen as guests began arriving. Everyone was advised Thanksgiving Dinner would be served outdoors in the Kiva.

As news of the fire sank in, instead of cancelling their reservations, guests pitched right in washing smoke-stained windows and helping with many other jobs. White Sun was their ranch, of course and it needed a lot of attention that day. Thanks to Jean and lots of helpers, Thanksgiving Dinner with all the trimmings was served in the Kiva!

Palm Springs pioneers Frank and Melba Bennett, of Deep Well Ranch, were our honored guests in 1957, at another Thanksgiving. Deep Well was the grandfather of the valley's guests ranches, and predated White Sun by seventeen years. Located at the mouth of the famous Indian Palm Canyon directly behind Palm Springs, the Bennetts insisted that Deep Well maintain natural desert landscaping and please, no lawns! Contrast that policy against today's 100 plus manicured golf courses and gated condominiums that have created a green belt from Palm Springs to Indio!

Frank and Melba Bennett's daughter, Mrs. Ralph B. (Deedee) Busch, Jr., of Santa Paula, California, gave me some Deep Well history in a letter dated July 2, 2000:

New Year's Eve celebrants decked out in Nancy's paper hats, are enjoying a feast, from left: Coleman and Jane Morton, Cindy, Derry and Dick Robinson; in foreground, Janie Morton, Annie Ward, Diana Morton and Winnie Robinson.

December 31, 1956
Jan Rouse Photo

I believe Deep Well was an apricot ranch in the early twenties, and the well, (there really was one!) was the deepest in the Coachella Valley at that time.

My father, business manager of the old Town House in Los Angeles, met Phil Boyd in the late twenties, in Palm Springs. Phil was a banker from the Midwest, and had moved to Palm Springs for his health, where he became Palm Springs' first mayor. He and Dorothy Marmon were the first Caucasian couple married there.

Dad and Phil Boyd purchased Deep Well in 1929, Phil was the silent financial partner and Dad was the manager. ... They could handle seventy-five guests, eventually, after adding two separate bedroom cottages.

During the Second World War my Dad was in the Air Force, so Mom ran the place by having half the rooms for guests, and the other half as temporary housing for various service men's families, until they could find other housing ... We were open all year during the war.

Alex, a new chef, took over the kitchen on one of Jean Schaffer's leaves. He was a stickler for delegating authority, which allowed him ample time to play shuffleboard with the guests, while his minions labored in the kitchen. On the sly, Alex played another game, supplying his wife with choice cuts of beef and hams for her small eatery in Indio, smuggled out of the ranch kitchen secreted in his trouser legs. Alex's tenure was short-lived.

I learned a different approach to cooking from our neighbors Barney and Vicki Gengenbach. A Brazilian from Sao Paulo, Vicki volunteered to coach me in the intricacies of Brazilian cuisine, since we were planning a Brazilian SITA Reunion with a Carnival theme. She came to my house in Palm Desert for a practice session. Lombo de Porco, Couve, Feijao, Farofa, Arroz, Batatas, all Greek to me!

"It's so easy, Helen!" Where had I heard those words before?

She settled herself comfortably on my kitchen stool and never left it. As if she had the full complement of maids from her Sao Paulo kitchen at her disposal, she gave directions and kept me running in circles. What sticks in my memory is the way she diced onions. Peel and slice an onion in half. Be sure the knife is sharp. Slice the half thinly, then rotate the onion and slice again. Now you are ready to cut across the grain for a perfect dice.

Peace and happiness did not always reign in the dining room. One morning purely by happenstance, five young couples sat down at the long table to breakfast together. None of them had met before. They found it easy to strike up friendships as people did at White Sun. All the wives were college educated except one, a gifted artist from Yugoslavia, dark-haired, dark-eyed and exceptionally pretty. One husband was a psychiatrist and they were soon discussing one of his cases. I noticed the artist never said a word.

Our wrangler Al Hein came around to sign up riders, jollying anyone who hesitated, encouraging them to come down to the stables and try out a gentle horse. The artist's husband motioned to me asking if we could talk in private. We walked around to my office in the lobby where he leaned over the counter whispering, "Please keep this confidential, Helen. Promise me you will not share it with anyone."

I couldn't imagine what was coming, but I nodded my head.

"My wife is trying to commit suicide and, well," he hesitated. "You see, I would like very much to go riding. Would you please keep an eye on her?"

What a tall order! Right there in the dining room sat a qualified psychiatrist who could have helped this poor, lost soul who felt herself so inferior to all those college graduates! I had promised not to breath a word but I was furious.

That morning lasted an eternity. When the riders finally returned I cornered the husband. "I'm sorry, sir, but I must ask you and your wife to leave."

He thanked me for his morning ride and shortly thereafter they checked

225

out. That was the only time I ever asked anyone to leave, although I came close one other time.

At the dinner table one evening, a woman was seated next to my five-year-old, Lissa. Something Lissa said or did, I no longer remember what, irritated the lady. In front of all the guests she sharply criticized her in a loud voice. I held my tongue with difficulty. It was unwarranted and cruel. Controlling my temper somehow, I let the moment pass, without adding fuel to the fire.

This guest in particular, was accustomed to room service, which we did not encourage, and heaven knows what else. She and her friends came to my desk after dinner, and under some pretext she blurted out,

"Oh I'm so very sorry, but we have to cancel our reservations. Something has come up."

Things have an amazing way of taking care of themselves! If people felt ill at ease at White Sun, they obviously didn't belong there. Most of them would adapt like the lady who dressed for dinner and wore a hat. She only did this once and quickly adjusted to our "laid-back," informal life-style. New Year's Eve was the time to go formal and they most certainly did with panache!

Another sample of White Sun "mystique." My first exposure to Hawaii with Jack was pure enchantment. How does anyone resist the charm of that lush, green world, the soothing guitars, languorous intoxication of waves, swaying hips and fragrant flowers? I was spellbound. I wanted to take it all home with me.

When we returned to the ranch we decided White Sun should have a Muu-muu Party. Hawaii's ideal garment is the Muu-muu, a loose, shapeless dress of bright colors and patterns that anyone can wear, effortless to slip on and great for hula dancing. In the 1950s we could buy flour sacks in bright colors and prints at any feed store, that easily converted to Muu-muus by cutting holes in the bottom and sides for your head and arms!

Staff chorus line kicks off a Muu-muu Party arrayed in flour sacks! Wrangler Al flaunts his bare legs, along with Jeanie Faulkner, Marianne, Nancy Carruthers, John and Bertha Phillips.

April 1953
Helen Dengler Photo

That was during the ranch's early days, when our guest and staff count was less than twenty. We had no problem finding enough flour sacks for everyone. Guests, staff, family, were all decked out in flour sack finery, with Al Hein, the wrangler, flashing bare, knobby knees. Posing for a picture just at that moment, some unexpected visitors walked in.

Arthur Keleher was one of our hula hussies and I watched him eyeball the strangers. There was a certain tilt to his eyebrows I recognized as negative. We all paraded around solemnly as the strangers stood at my check-in counter, looking non-plussed.

They didn't stand very long. Slowly they turned around and filed out the door.

Bella Bella the ranch mascot joins the Muu-muu Party.

April 1953
Helen Dengler Photo

Author of THE NUN STORY, Katherine Hulme enjoys a ride to the sand dunes on my favorite, Black Hawk.

December 1955
Al Hein Photo

chapter 16

White Sun Kaleidoscope

Postum did not seem an appropriate beverage for White Sun. This innocuous breakfast drink, totally devoid of caffeine, was part of the Dykema morning ritual when I was growing up in Madison, Wisconsin. I even inflicted it on Jack, who never complained when we first set up housekeeping in a small Manhattan apartment. My father abhorred coffee as well as smoking, alcohol, and perfume. Woe betide the poor soul aspiring to be Professor Dykema's secretary if Dad detected the merest whiff of perfume. That hopeful soul was surely covering up something worse. As for coffee, I was told to wait an interminable forty years before tasting a cup!

Mother set a different example. She was the exception in the family, serenely defying Dad's warnings. She brazenly sipped her coffee every morning until she died, at the age of 88.

I broke the rules and tasted my first cup of coffee at White Sun three years shy of my fortieth birthday. I found hot coffee a great ice breaker. If guests checked in before a room was ready, I'd suggest, "Would you like a cup of coffee?" What better way to get acquainted and ease them into the ranch ambience.

One day two middle-aged women walked briskly up to my desk. Leaning over the counter the shorter of the two asked for a quiet room where they would not be disturbed. "I'm in mid-book," she informed me, introducing herself as Katherine Hulme. By "mid-book" she was referring to THE NUN'S STORY. (After its publication and popular success, it inspired the award-winning 1959 Hollywood movie starring Audrey Hepburn and Peter Finch.)

Katherine turned to her companion, introducing her as Lou Habets and explained Lou was the real nun of the book's story. Time for coffee! We got acquainted. Then I showed them several rooms until they were satisfied with one far enough away from the pool. After they were settled, Katherine donned her English riding habit and headed straight for the stables.

White Sun offered many activities: horseback riding, archery, badminton, basketball, bicycles, a children's playhouse and pool with bridges connecting a little island in its middle, golf, a game room, horseshoe pitching, a hot tub and sauna, paddle tennis, ping pong, shuffleboard, square dancing, three swimming pools, five tennis courts, and volleyball. (No partridge in a pear tree, only mocking birds on the roof!) Guests could pick and choose but frequently favored none of the above! They liked having everything available, but sun-tanning in lounge chairs by one of the heated pools often seemed the most appealing.

It took a little effort to climb out of a lounge chair in response to the old ranch bell announcing lunch or dinner, but Jean Schaffer's meals were too appetizing to miss!

In the Round-Up Bar, the Happy Hour had come and gone. "The Horrible Hour," as Arthur Keleher termed it, followed dinner. What to do next? Most guests quickly figured that out, playing games in the lobby, or taking off for a moonlight ride to the sand dunes with Al Hein or Ed Burrus. Glamorous, intriguing Palm Springs was nearby. Why not an evening at the Chi Chi Club where Nat King Cole might be singing? A big hit during the fifties was THE GAME, similar to charades, which provided guests, like Alice Brush, with a lot of after-dinner fun.

She and her husband, Major General Rapp Brush just happened on the ranch one afternoon, like Cliff and Ruth Powers, and decided to stay a few days. After those few days passed, Rapp and Alice decided to stay a month. Soon they were part of our ranch family. How lucky for us! They returned every year in spring, always for a month or two. "The Iggies are coming!" we'd say. "The Iggies are on their way!" The Iggies were an unusually close and devoted couple. During World War II when Rapp served with General Douglas MacArthur in the South Pacific, he and Alice kept in touch by cable using the code word "Iggy," a habit they continued after the war.

One day Alice invited me to join them for a drink and asked, "Would you please bring along your accordion?" I was happy to oblige. I told her I'd meet them in the bar at five o'clock.

232

Farewell party for two very special guests, Major General Rapp and Alice Brush from Menlo Park, California.

January 1957
Jan Rouse Photo

Oh no! I had misunderstood. The bar was not part of the General's protocol. I was to bring my accordion to his room. Since it would not do to refuse a command performance, I agreed, but made it clear this would be a one time only exception to White Sun's protocol!

After that very private experience I was all the more surprised one evening when Alice joined us in the lobby where we were playing THE GAME. Someone from two opposing teams steps forward to pantomime the words in the title of a book, movie, play, or song, first using hand signals to announce his or her chosen category, then the number of words in the title. The opposing team must correctly guess the title.

Alice impressed us immediately with her remarkable stage presence and dramatic ability. This elegant, refined, very private lady turned into an extrovert before our eyes. She became an enthusiastic player, but her gallant, twinkly-eyed General Rapp chose to be a spectator and just watch the show.

Down-to-earth folks, movie stars Henry (Biff) and Joan Wilcoxon discovered White Sun in the fifties and made it a habit. Joannie dazzled us amidst the Saturday night square dancers and Biff got a kick out of playing White Sun bartender back in the days when we only had a private bottle bar.

On one of his many rides out to the sand dunes, Biff came across an abandoned stand-pipe in the sand. He dismounted to experiment with the pipe's acoustics and made a startling discovery. He had located the voice of Moses! At the time, Biff was Associate Producer of Cecil B. DeMille's film in progress, THE TEN COMMANDMENTS. When Biff returned to Hollywood he convinced DeMille that he had found the voice of Moses in our back-yard!

In due course the Paramount Studio flatbed trucks arrived, loaded with equipment and crew, girls in bathing suits (technicians?) and Charlton Heston. But the truck drivers, no doubt inadvertently, had not anticipated driving on sand. The stand-pipe lay half a mile off the paved road and that last half mile was loose desert sand. The bikini girls acquired a great suntan while the drivers worked out their dilemma!

Jack sports a charro suit for square dance night with partner Joan Wilcoxon.

December 1956
Helen Dengler Photo

Movie star Biff Wilcoxon joins travel agents Dorothy Patterson, Jody Foss and acting bartender Robert Van der Sloot in the cozy Round-Up Bar.

May 19,1956
Jan Rouse Photo

DeMille's 1923 silent version of THE TEN COMMANDMENTS cost Paramount Studios over a million dollars, then considered outrageous. His 1956 color/sound remake cost well over thirteen million dollars and won only the Academy Award Oscar for Best Special Effects. We like to think Biff Wilcoxon's desert expedition to record Heston's voice in the stand-pipe contributed a small yet vital part in winning that award! Four White Sun regulars were featured in the film, Yul Brynner (Rameses, the Pharoah), Henry Wilcoxon (Pentaur), Dotty Neumann (a slave girl), and Joan Wilcoxon (a high priestess).

Another White Sun regular, Marian Sweeney lived in a wheel chair, handicapped from early childhood with polio. Both her legs were useless. But nobody believed she was truly handicapped. Her lively eyes missed nothing, dancing with the polka and square dancers or galloping along with the horseback riders. She delighted in all ranch activities. From the start White Sun measured up surprisingly well to present-day handicap specifications. Marian deftly wheeled her chair over the ranch's level walkways and patios and seemed just like everyone else, part of the action.

Blanche Vanstrom, a frequent guest, checked in one day in a wheel chair also, her broken leg in a cast. Blanche and her husband Van were both ardent, stylish horseback riders but this was Blanche's first experience riding a wheel chair. She tried keeping up with Marian but with little success. Long since Marian had mastered wheel chair locomotion. Blanche could take comfort knowing she'd be back on her feet, and back on a horse in the not-too-distant future

The ranch often served as effective therapy for guests who needed rest, sunshine, and care. It certainly helped one hen-pecked husband who arrived for a week's stay. His wife had made the reservation, explaining he was suffering from depression and needed a change. She would be down to fetch him on the weekend. The gentleman discovered our set of traps in the bar and asked if there was any objection to his playing the drums. We told him to please go right ahead. So every day he happily drummed

Marian Sweeney feasts her eyes on the desert's lavender sand verbena and evening primrose, magically sprouting after a spring rain.

March 26, 1964
Helen Dengler Photo

238

*Van and Blanche Vanstrom tried out a Hawaiian holiday but decided
to come back where they belonged.*

October 1968
Helen Dengler Photo

239

away, getting noticeably better and brighter. By the time his wife arrived, he was excited and eager to demonstrate his new accomplishments.

"What on earth do you think you're doing?" she demanded. She insisted he quit this childish behavior at once and return home with her. Who wouldn't be depressed!

Sam, one of our groundskeepers had other problems, car problems. Every day he had a long commute to work from Banning, up in the pass. Sam needed a reliable car and the wreck he owned was always breaking down. He asked Si Slocum about getting a loan for a car replacement. Si checked out the used car market and found Sam a fuel efficient car in excellent condition, a yellow station wagon. Sam was dismayed. He had something else in mind, some big, impressive, sleek-finned gas guzzler, something that would satisfy his wife and kids, like a Cad?

"Sam, you can't afford a big car," Si cautioned. "It burns a lot of gas." Si was patient and persuasive. Finally he convinced Sam to buy the yellow wagon.

Our insurance agent Ray Lusby was Sam's next hurdle. If the ranch was to advance him a loan on the car, it had to be insured. Lusby met Sam in the SITA office.

"May I see your license, Sam?" Lusby held out his hand. Sam began a slow, methodical search of all his pockets. Nothing turned up. All his life Sam had been driving without a license!

Lusby smiled. "Well now Sam, first you'll have to take a driver's license test."

At this point, Sunday Martin appeared. Tall, husky Sunday and his wife Gloria worked in the ranch kitchen. Sunday graciously offered to drive Sam to Palm Springs to take the driver's test. Sam was stubborn and still determined to fight the whole process. Bowing his head, he finally muttered, "I can't read."

Big Sunday smiled encouragement. That's no problem. Sam could get

At the Tahitian Reunion Lynn Morgan presents neighbor "Kanakakai" Hank Gogerty with the Most Talented Prize for his hula dancing.

January 21, 1961
Palm Springs LIFE Photo

241

around that since they gave oral driver's tests on Wednesdays!

The very next Wednesday Sam and Sunday drove in to Palm Springs. Sam passed the test with flying colors. The yellow station wagon was his!

After some rocky beginnings, our neighbor Hank Gogerty had come around to sharing his Desert Air Hotel landing strip with us. This was a large plus for our fly-in guests like Lee Crager, who could walk directly from his Luscomb plane, tied down at our front gate, to his White Sun room. Next Gogerty invited us to one of his luaus at Desert Air Hotel. Neighborly relations were on the upswing. To our surprise Hank's hula dancing at the luau was the hit of the evening!

When the SITA Tahitian Reunion was scheduled at the ranch, it was our turn to send Gogerty an invitation. This grey-haired, prominent Los Angeles architect and businessman arrived at the party attired in a pareo, (a Tahitian wrap-around skirt,) slung low over his hips, a flower over his ear and little else. Under his bushy eyebrows his eyes sparkled with delight as he swiveled his way center stage, a bright red light flashing on and off in his navel!

We had had serious disagreements with Gogerty in the past, regarding planes taking off too low over power lines on Magnesia Falls Drive, our access road. How can you be angry with a guy flashing a red light in his belly button? We re-routed the power lines.

True Slocum can tell Joe Noster's story better than anyone. When the Slocums became our ranch managers, they brought Joe along as a bartender.

True remembers ... "Everybody liked Joe and would go to see him as a friend, rather than a bartender. Some guests would sit there in the cozy little bar a long time just to be with Joe and hear his loud 'Hee Haw!' He was such a marvelous dancer too. Whenever there was something going on, somebody's birthday, or Saturday Night Steak-Fry ... when the dance

Joe Noster, everyone's favorite bar-tender.

1965
Courtesy Shirley P. Jones

music came on, Joe would dance with you. Even if you weren't a good dancer Joe would make you one, he was such a strong leader."

"Bar-tending was his 'moonlight' job. Daytimes he was a builder and a painter, and he would also do remodeling for friends. He added on an apartment to my little house in Rancho Mirage. He would do anything for a friend and always tried to save you money."

"We first met Joe at the Lone Palm Hotel in Palm Springs," True explained, "... soon after he got out of the service. He had fought in the Battle of the Bulge and was very lucky to have come home! 'Oh, we had a blast! ...' Joe hee-hawed."

"Joe gained our respect immediately. He would do anything, bell-man, you name it ... Being an independent builder he could be 'on call,' a tremendous help to any hotel operator."

True waxed nostalgic: "One of our pet guests at White Sun, Clara de Lendrecie who was in her eighties, was very fond of Joe. He was one of the drawing cards that brought her back to the ranch year after year. She and I stayed up with Joe, just the three of us until 4 A.M. to celebrate one New Year's Eve, just talking and laughing at Clara who could come up with the funniest remarks, captivating her audience. ... Yes, everybody liked Joe. We'd see him coming always when he said he would, and we knew we were in for a good time at the bar."

Desert Protective Council officers for 1970 hold a board meeting at White Sun, from left: Dr. Henry M. Weber, Associate Executive Director; Jane Pinheiro, Treasurer; Robert Bear, Executive Director; Dr. Robin Ives, Vice President; Helen Dengler, Secretary; and Tasker Edmiston, President.

January 17, 1970
Photo Courtesy DPC's Harriet Allen

chapter 17

Move Over Fella

My fearless friend Dr. Henry M.Weber, president of the Desert Protective Council from 1967 to 1969, could sweet-talk venomous snakes into doing his bidding, and on occasion even members of the Riverside County Board of Supervisors. One lovely spring day in 1968, I joined Weber and other members of the DPC on a Santa Rosa Mountain hike. The narrow, precipitous trail led sharply around a bend. Weber was in the lead and discovered a coiled rattlesnake sunning itself, completely blocking our path. He paused, then in a gentle, reasonable way he requested,

"Move over fella, and let us pass."

Much to my amazement, the rattler uncoiled itself and slithered away. With no further comment, we all continued around the bend.

I had joined the Desert Protective Council in 1967, at the urging of its executive director, Bob Bear and my Palm Desert neighbor Randall Henderson, the distinguished publisher and editor of DESERT MAGAZINE. DPC was founded October 23, 1954, to preserve the integrity of Joshua Tree National Monument originally, now fully protected as a National Park, thanks to the efforts of the DPC, among others. DPC's charter members, nine men and one woman started out with this slogan, which has never been altered:

"To safeguard for wise and reverent use by this and succeeding generations, those desert areas of unique, scenic, scientific, historical, spiritual and recreational value, and to educate by all appropriate means children and adults to a better understanding of the desert."

DPC's primary founder and first president was Harry C. James. He had come to the United States from Ottawa, Canada, in 1915, and soon after organized a conservation club for boys featuring camping trips in the West. This led to the founding of his TRAILFINDERS SCHOOL FOR BOYS in 1926, combining education with wilderness trips. James focused on the American

West, the big outdoors. He authored a number of successful books on the Hopi and Cahuilla Indians.

Trailfinders acquired 26 acres for their school in the San Jacinto Mountains in 1941, including Lolomi Lodge,[1] which became Harry's and his wife Grace Clifford James' retirement home. Several times I drove Randall Henderson's wife Cyria, up to the Lodge to visit the James. During one of these visits, Harry told me the story of a book he had been writing.

He and Grace had been warned of a serious forest fire coming their way and were told to evacuate immediately. Thinking the safest way to protect his manuscript was to bury it, Harry placed all his papers in a metal box, hurriedly dug a deep hole, and covered it with dirt. The fire came close but spared Lolomi Lodge. However, the intense heat of the blaze ignited a nearby tree's roots. The burning roots led to Harry's hole and his box, and completely incinerated his manuscript!

To become a member of such an enlightened, stimulating group as the Desert Protective Council's Board of Directors, was my privilege. "By all appropriate means" they most certainly educated me "to a better understanding of the desert."

President James' deprecatory humor in the following quote, is typical of the organization, printed in DPC's first newsletter in the spring of 1955:

Volume I—Number 1

EL PAISANO, the roadrunner, seems a fitting name for a newsletter, which will be issued with considerable irregularity. We hope that, like its namesake, it will be on the job when some particularly poisonous reptile—some genuine threat to the purposes of the Desert Protective Council—coils to strike. I can only hope that EL PAISANO's relation to birds of the cuckoo family will not be too obvious to our readers.

Public hearings were to become part of my life. Dr. Weber demonstrated his way to handle them. The good doctor, who was fairly deaf, often turned off his hearing aid during these lengthy proceedings. Giving the appearance of a polite, attentive listener, he patiently waited his turn at the microphone.

In response to "Are there any further comments?" Weber would step up to the mike, graciously addressing the Board, the lawyers, the pro and con factions, making us all feel like one big, happy family. Never raising his voice, just as he had addressed the rattlesnake, he would argue scientifically and convincingly for the environment. As often as possible, whether relevant or irrelevant, he would insinuate into his comments his firm stand against the hunting of doves during their nesting season. Then he would quietly withdraw to his chair.

In Palm Desert, I signed up for an evening birding class, taught by another founding DPC member, Dr. Ernest Tinkham. He lectured on Desert Life and Lost Gold Mines at College of the Desert, and he was in the midst of writing a book on Roadrunners. One night he brought his pet roadrunner, "Roady," to class. He explained to us how the bird had bonded with him, and actually considered Tinkham his mate, perching on Tinkham's head and bending down to offer him nesting materials.

Roadrunners are large birds. Though slender they have strong legs and feet and a remarkable 11-inch tail. Unrestricted in our classroom, Roady flew straight to the one student clearly frightened of him and perched on her arm. As she drew back in fear, Tinkham gently called his pet and the bird flew back to him at once.

Intentionally built loosely out of sticks, it looks like a clumsy affair, but a roadrunner's nest provides the clutch of three to six eggs with some natural air-conditioning in the desert heat. Our favorite roadrunner built one in the giant tamarisk tree shading our White Sun patio. Another DPC member, photographer Hans Baerwald, brought his camera and perched on a ladder for two hours, patiently waiting to get the perfect shot of the nesting bird.

Roadrunners are members of the cuckoo family and are mostly ground-fast, although they can fly fifty to a hundred yards at a time. Typically seen in the desert or other dry open areas, they are also known as "paisano" (fellow-countryman), chaparral cock, snake-bird, chorea (or churella) and corella de camino. At lunch one day at White Sun, a new guest from Yonkers, New York, added one more colorful description:

"Guess what, folks? I've just seen my first 'street walker'!"

Other birds fly away when scared but roadrunners just dart off on the ground, streamlined head thrust forward, crest flattened, tail streaking out behind. When they stop the crest goes erect, head turning this way and that to check on potential enemies.

Just what was I doing joining forces with a "potential enemy" like the Desert Protective Council? This organization was dedicated to the preservation of the desert and all its wildlife, including those scorpions that had given me such a scare in 1946! My "about-face" had been gradual, transforming me from that once suspicious female for whom all deserts were anathema, into a desert activist! DPC played a significant role in my conversion.

Since our family's arrival in Southern California in 1941, I had been a Sierra Club member, but hardly an activist. We simply enjoyed hiking and work parties on Mt. Baldy. Then along came my 1950s decade of running White Sun, when I was all but blind to the world outside that magical oasis. I had no time or energy left to participate in local affairs or to become a joiner.

When we moved from White Sun to more privacy in Rancho Mirage's neighboring town, Palm Desert, during the tumultuous sixties, my focus changed dramatically. We found a home on Old Prospector Trail but a stone's throw from legendary desert advocate Randall Henderson and his sculptress wife, Cyria. I began a new life.

Over at White Sun, Si and True Slocum inherited my manager's office, the problems, crises and all my pending baggage. I could take off my blinders. I could explore the world around me with different eyes. And I became a joiner in earnest!

Desert Beautiful was first on my list. Randall Henderson's brother Cliff,

Volunteer Litter Drive in action. Eloise Dunphy drives Fincher Contractors' pick-up for Rancho Mirage Desert Beautiful. On Saturdays adults and children fan out over roads and highways with donated trucks, to clean up the desert and recycle all usable items.

April 1963
Helen Dengler Photo

the founder of Palm Desert, had married a glamorous movie star, Marian Marsh. Soon after she arrived in the desert, Marian attended a meeting where the speaker was the famous flyer Jackie Cochran, the first woman to break the sound barrier, who ranted and raved about desert litter, so apparent from the air. Marian began paying attention and resolved to do something about that! In 1961 she founded Desert Beautiful, which she has effectively guided for over forty years.

Marian Henderson personified Desert Beautiful. Not only glamorous, she was eloquent, skillful and most persuasive. I volunteered to be Rancho Mirage Desert Beautiful chairman. We got busy organizing clean-up drives, mobilizing kids in the neighborhood, my family, and businessmen with pick-up trucks. After the drives, White Sun provided refreshments for the hot, thirsty workers. To beautify our local post office we organized a "Memory Lane" drive, planted trees, and dedicated the finished project to commemorate Rancho Mirage's pioneers with fanfare and a handsome plaque.

Next I became secretary of the Rancho Mirage Chamber of Commerce. In my almost lifetime capacity as SITA's Public Relations Director, I had all of SITA's office and print shop facilities on the ranch at my disposal, very handy for a secretary! My first order of business was to design a Chamber of Commerce brochure with a map of Rancho Mirage, funded by local businesses.[2]

After lengthy discussions with my neighbor Randall Henderson, I urged the Chamber to promote Magnesia Falls Canyon as a park or nature preserve for the endangered Peninsula bighorn sheep (ovis canadensis), once numerous in the area. Bighorn were federally listed as endangered in 1998. In early days, Cahuilla Indians called the canyon "Pahwah-te" (The Drinker), and it is also known as Magnesia Springs Canyon. Rancho Mirage is built on the broad, alluvial fan below Magnesia Falls Canyon, which drains a watershed area of about 5 ¼ square miles.

I created White Sun's ORDER OF THE BIGHORN SOCIETY to discourage encroaching development into bighorn habitat, and trophy hunting (which

Desert Beautiful chairman Marian Henderson visits Magnesia Falls Canyon with Helen, to check out its potential as a wildlife reserve.

December 1963
Helen Dengler Photo

BE IT KNOWN UNTO ALL MEN

that in this Modern Age of Scientific Achievement and Economic
Growth, — within view of the expanding resort communities of
Southern California's Coachella Valley,

_____ sighted_____

DESERT BIGHORN SHEEP (OVIS CANADENSIS)

in_____ near_____

on the____day of_____, accompanied by_____
and is hereby officially inducted into the

ORDER OF THE BIGHORN

SOCIETY
of WHITE SUN GUEST RANCH

RANCHO MIRAGE, CALIFORNIA 92270, U.S.A.
In witness whereof this certificate has been duly signed
by WHITE SUN BIGHORN GUARDIANS:

Nº   377

Date:
Rancho Mirage, Calif.

White Sun's ORDER OF THE BIGHORN SOCIETY certificate was
awarded individuals who could prove sighting Bighorn Sheep with
a witness or a photo.

February 1964
Designed by DESERT MAGAZINE's Al Merryman

254

continued even though California gave the sheep protected status in 1873); to alert the public to the bighorn's threatened status; and to experience the thrill of observing and photographing them.

Two of our ranch guests became the first Bighorn Society members in February 1964, when Jean Trocme, the San Francisco French Consul General's Commercial Counselor and his wife Pat spotted three bighorn sheep above Palm Desert, near the Palms-to-Pines Highway. Anyone was eligible for a lifetime membership who had proof of spotting a bighorn, together with a witness, or with photographic evidence.

Bighorn Society members were rewarded with a handsome certificate illustrated with the head of a bighorn ram, designed by DESERT MAGAZINE's Al Merryman. During the ten years of its existence, membership in The Order of the Bighorn Society grew to 377 individuals. When Rancho Mirage was incorporated, on August 3, 1973, the city adopted the bighorn ram as its symbol.

A year after joining the Desert Protective Council in 1967, I was appointed to a two-year term on the Riverside County Park Advisory Commission and became its chairman. On November 14, 1968 Randall Henderson[3] wrote me as follows:

> I want to congratulate you and Riverside County as well, on your appointment to the Park Advisory Commission. I have long felt that this committee needed someone with your enthusiasm and initiative to put a stick of dynamite under the upholstered chair of Edward Walker, who has done virtually nothing during the eight years he has drawn a salary as County Parks Director.

> But please forget the prejudice I have expressed and give him the benefit of the doubt, until you have had time to form your own opinion as to his competence.

With Randall's encouragement I invited Park Director Ed Walker and Riverside County Administrator, Robert Anderson (who later became a DPC member), to visit Magnesia Falls Canyon with me and biology researcher

Hoping to enlist Riverside County Parks Director Ed Walker and Riverside County Administrator Robert Anderson in a drive to preserve Magnesia Falls Canyon, biologist Lloyd Tevis and Helen invited them for an early morning visit to the canyon. We lucked out, surprising a band of seven bighorn sheep above the bare rock falls.

June 1964
Helen Dengler Photo

Lloyd Tevis, yet another distinguished DPC member and long-time friend. On a June morning we trekked up to the canyon mouth and surprised seven bighorn, including three lambs, at the top of the great rock falls. Clutching his binoculars, Walker ran to the wall as if defying gravity to ascend in one giant leap. The bighorns vanished.

His sole comment was, "Helen, you let them out of a box!"

Walker was replaced by the brilliant new County Parks Director and landscape architect, Pete Dangermond, who later became California State Parks Director. He now heads his own land planning company, the multi-faceted Dangermond Group devoted to parks, recreation, tourism, allied fields of wildlife conservation and open space preservation. Pete blew our minds he was so far ahead of us. He challenged us to think with a broader, regional outlook. Lake Cahuilla County Park at the terminus of the All American Canal was one of many projects our Commission achieved under his direction. Public hearings became an endless and vital part of this job and I hadn't forgotten Dr. Weber's strategy.

Involvement in one group generally leads to another, this time member-ship in THE LIVING DESERT founded in 1971, by Palm Springs' first mayor Philip L. Boyd, with Lucien Shaw its first president. On the recommendation of the Arizona-Sonora Desert Museum, Living Desert's Board of Directors chose a most enterprising, remarkable, and totally dedicated young woman, Karen Sausman as its first Executive Director. During the past thirty years, Karen earned the highest respect, worldwide, for developing and expanding the Living Desert. Both Lloyd Tevis and I, though no longer active, are still listed among the Living Desert's honorary directors.

Just for fun, without any public hearings or secretarial duties, I joined my dear friend Barbara Patterson on weekly outings with Dr. Milton Walker's un-titled desert hiking seniors. Barbara, a transplanted down-easterner from Maine living in nearby Bermuda Dunes, had become an ardent desert devo-tee and Sierra Club leader. She and Walker's jolly bunch of senior citizens were in far better physical shape than I. They put me to shame with their vertical climbing talents, as well as vertical canyon descents!

Lloyd Tevis explains how earthquake fault lines, by damming ground water and forcing it to the surface, create oases that supply food and water for desert fauna and flora. Here Washingtonia filifera native palms thrive with their "petticoat skirts" that insulate the trunks and offer habitat for a variety of insects and birds.

Magnesia Falls Canyon
January 1964
Helen Dengler Photo

I soon learned the unspoken condition for joining the group was a strict boycott on any discussion regarding politics or religion. Walker was a wild-flower expert, familiar with the Latin names of every cactus or belly-flower we came across. Among the others, Ray McCarty and Peppy Campbell were regular mountain goats with unlimited energy and years of familiarity with the desert terrain. On one of our steepest ascents Marian Rosher, at least fifteen years my senior, strode uphill behind me as if she were on level ground, and politely asked: "Do you mind if I walk through, Helen?"

Everyone was equipped with state-of-the-art hiking gear. Descending Palm Canyon, they leapt from boulder to boulder, secure in their Italian hiking boots. I was wearing tennis shoes but they were far too polite to comment. I landed on a rock that slanted backwards and nearly broke my ankle. I kept this to myself managing to limp all the way down, vowing to invest in a stout pair of boots before any more hikes and no more tennis shoes!

On another long traverse in the Santa Rosas, we exited again through Palm Canyon. Heat and weariness made my slow pace obvious to a couple of little children who spotted me limping toward our cars. The smaller child called after me, "Tender feet?"

Be that as it may, I eagerly looked forward to these weekly explorations that improved my fitness and knowledge of the desert. On hot days we headed up to Idyllwild in the mountains, and on cool winter days down to the Mecca Hills' tortuous, winding canyons.

There were no cliques in the group. I found each hiker a mine of information as well as a pleasant companion. There was an added bonus: Dr. Walker's wife, Helen, (I called her Patty,) had studied piano in Vienna and she found time to play piano duets with me almost every week.

Being a joiner did not mean neglecting my duties at the ranch, which was just a short drive from our Palm Desert home. I still spent a good part of the week in the SITA office composing WHITE SUN ROUND-UPS or SITAGRAMS, just part of my public relations activities. Like SITA alumni, White Sun guests too became members of our extended family. I was on call for Scrabble, square dancing, guiding desert outings, accordion sessions in the bar, at steak-fries and chuck wagon breakfasts.

Keeping fit and happy, members of Dr. Milton Walker's senior hiking group become intimately acquainted with the desert's hidden treasures. From left: Ray McCarty, Barbara Patterson (who invited me to join), Pete Kahn, Helen and Peppy Campbell, kneeling.

Horse Thief Canyon
October 1973
Dr. Milton Walker Photo

*Exploring the labyrinth of Mecca Hills'
passageways south of Indio, Dr. Walker
is first to emerge, followed by Marian
Rosher, Chuck Reddan (beard), Peppy
Campbell, Helen, Ray McCarty and
Ruth Seaman.*

Ladder Canyon
November 1973
Pete Kahn Photo

A desert bighorn sheep family, Ovis Canadensis.

Ralph Welles Photo

Wrangler Ed Burrus grabs the cable to lead guests up the steep rock face of Magnesia Falls Canyon.

December 1963
Helen Dengler Photo

★ ★ ★

No one played a larger role in opening my eyes to Magnesia Falls Canyon and the plight of the bighorn sheep, than David. Ever since he was a small boy, David had been a keen observer of nature. When he went abroad at age thirteen, for a year of schooling in the glorious Swiss Alps, he told me, much later, "… Switzerland had a lot to do with it."

When he returned to White Sun from the Ecole d'Humanité, David spent free time exploring desert canyons, the closest being Magnesia Falls. He became such a familiar part of their landscape, the bighorn paid no attention to him and he could study them at close range.

David told me his remarkable science teacher at Coachella Valley Union High School, David MacKaye, was the one "who made us THINK!" MacKaye routinely took his students out of the classroom to study desert flora and fauna. In the classroom, MacKaye insisted on scholarship and dedication to taxonomy. Note taking was lengthy and painstaking. In fact some parents complained about MacKaye because their teenagers stayed up so late doing his homework assignments!

Someone had fastened a cable to facilitate climbing up the dry rock falls that guard the entrance to Magnesia Falls Canyon. David encouraged me to try it and find what he had discovered in the canyon: a chrysocolla mine; miners' mule paths; groves of *Washingtonia filifera*, fan palm oases formed by earthquake fault lines which force groundwater to the surface; and grinding holes in flat rocks, mute evidence of Cahuilla Indian encampments. The canyon was narrow and convoluted, great terrain for bighorn. For those hardy White Sunners willing to climb it, Magnesia Falls provided a great adventure.

★ ★ ★

Explosive urban development in the Coachella Valley during the 1980s was rapidly encroaching on the mountains, intensifying efforts by many different groups and individuals to protect this vital, scenic area. These organizations included long-time advocate the Desert Protective Council, the Bureau of Land Management, California Department of Fish and Game, Wildlife Conservation Board, Riverside County, Friends of the Desert

264

Mountains, Coachella Valley Mountains Conservancy, the Indian tribes and cities within the valley.

I wrote Pete Dangermond about the status of Magnesia Falls Canyon preservation efforts in the Santa Rosa Mountains. He replied February 27, 1999:

> Virtually the entire drainage area is in public ownership, thanks in no small way to the efforts and directions you helped establish. Only two small segments of two sections remain at the very upper end, next to the Dunn Road.

> Mike Dunn (an ardent developer) passed away a couple of years ago but before he died, he saw most of the lands he dreamed about developing, become publicly owned.

On October 24, 2000, President Clinton signed legislation designating 272,000 acres of the Santa Rosa and San Jacinto Mountains a National Monument, now officially named the Santa Rosa and San Jacinto Mountains National Monument. The new designation expanded by 80,000 acres what was previously the Santa Rosa Mountains National Scenic Area, created March 31, 1990. Parts of the Agua Caliente Indian Reservation and portions of the San Bernardino National Forest are now included in the Monument, as well as Magnesia Falls Canyon!

After my twenty-six year stint in the desert, the last five as a DPC member, I was elected president of the Desert Protective Council for 1972–1973. However, my term in office lasted only a year, before my Long Island sailor Jack shanghaied me away to live on South Padre Island, on the Texas coast. To relinquish all my desert commitments was heart wrenching. I knew very well once Jack completed an undertaking to his satisfaction, the game was over. White Sun had ceased to be a challenge. The ranch no longer needed Denglers in person. It functioned smoothly by remote control with tried and true, competent management and staff, fully developed amenities, and a long list of loyal, repeat customers.

Jack had sold SITA, his first highly successful business, in 1969. Ten years later he was ready to sell his world famous guest ranch, White Sun.

Just kick off those old cowboy boots and slip into sneakers! The Gulf of Mexico's tempting blue waters offered a yachtsman very different challenges from a desert!

Far from settling down to a quiet life of retirement on the Texas coast, Jack embarked on yet another enterprise and returned to his first love, the boat business. Our six little Denglers were grown and scattered from coast to coast.

High time for me to cultivate my garden and get on with writing!

Roblay's Elegy

Lorgnettes or no lorgnettes
It's very plain to see
I have a hatfull of regrets
To leave, and ne'er to be
Excited, daft, bewitched, beguiled
By Denglers sane or Denglers wild
(But never tame, and never mild.)
And oh! The Dengler talents!
There was music every moment
For the staff and for the guest
There was hammering and riveting
To soothe the savage breast.
Guitar, harmonica—just say it.
The Denglers sing, the Denglers play it.
Alas, now life for me
A void so boring, dull and drear
I'll never be the same again,
Without that ever lovin' cheer.

White Sun farewell!
The clanging bell,
The dying knell.
White Sun, farewell!

Roblay McMullen, White Sun's poet laureate and an interim manager, operates her own Lake Creek Lodge resort in Sisters, Oregon in summer.

December 1958
Helen Dengler Photo

267

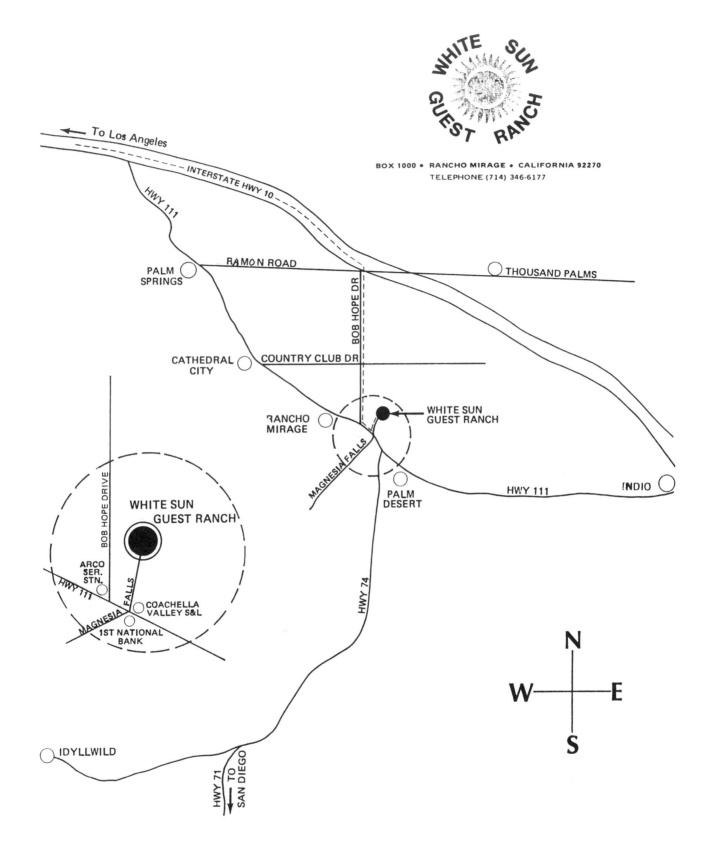

To Los Angeles

INTERSTATE HWY 10

HWY 111

RAMON ROAD

PALM SPRINGS

THOUSAND PALMS

BOB HOPE DR

CATHEDRAL CITY

COUNTRY CLUB DR

WHITE SUN GUEST RANCH

RANCHO MIRAGE

MAGNESIA FALLS

PALM DESERT

HWY 111

INDIO

BOB HOPE DRIVE

WHITE SUN GUEST RANCH

ARCO SER. STN.

HWY 111

MAGNESIA FALLS

COACHELLA VALLEY S&L

1ST NATIONAL BANK

HWY 74

N
W — E
S

IDYLLWILD

HWY 71 TO SAN DIEGO

1975 Area map of the Coachella Valley

268

Notes

Foreword

Note to page vii

1. Marking the end of an era, White Sun Guest Ranch burns to the ground 45 and a half years after its 1946 founding. Palm Springs DESERT SUN newspaper reports the story.

Chapter 1—The Awesome Desert

Notes to pages 1, 4, and 6

1. Tony Burke, a transplanted Englishman and camera buff, was the agent who sold The Eleven Mile Ranch to Jack Dengler in 1946. Tony had arrived in the Palm Springs area in 1929. In the forward to Tony Burke's 1978 book, PALM SPRINGS WHY I LOVE YOU, Bing Crosby described Burke as "… unusual, vastly entertaining … in no time Tony is clicking away, first in Los Angeles and Hollywood, then in 'America's Foremost Desert Resort,' Palm Springs. His snapshot microcosms, along with his public-relations inventiveness, did much to shape the history of Palm Springs, and bring prosperity and fame to the Little Village."

2. For at least 3,000 years the Cahuilla Indians were the original inhabitants of the Cathedral City area. But it was Colonel Henry Washington (U.S. Corps of Engineers) who first named a canyon in the mountains behind the little town, Cathedral Canyon. That was back in 1850. The canyon looked to him like the interior of a great cathedral. But it wasn't until developers put in the first subdivision that it was called Cathedral City, and incorporation to true city status did not come until 1981.

The Desert Sun

VALLEY

A3

Inside:

On the record / A4
Across the valley / A4-5
News from back home / A6

White Sun Guest Ranch clubhouse burns

Abandoned resort slated to be torn down

TUESDAY, November 26, 1991
Tom Tait, City Editor: 778-4620

DAN MacMEDAN/The Desert Sun

By ROSE WOJNAR
The Desert Sun

RANCHO MIRAGE — Fire destroyed the clubhouse of the abandoned White Sun Guest Ranch Monday, a historic resort that catered to Hollywood stars of three decades.

The noontime fire sent smoke billowing over the Coachella Valley, and some roads were snarled with motorists looking at the blaze.

The two-alarm fire leveled the 45-year-old, 10,000-square-foot clubhouse, but 35 firefighters stopped it from burning adjacent buildings housing 72 rooms.

All buildings are to be demolished to make way for 67 single-family homes to be built on 18 acres of the 60-acre ranch, but no date has been scheduled for the razing, said Bob Kleiman, senior vice president of Braemar, a development company based in Agoura. The fire shouldn't help or hinder the project, he said.

Riverside County firefighters used the fact the buildings are to be demolished in their battle, said Battalion Chief Mike McConnell.

Instead of risking lives to save an

270

Site of dude ranch was desert hot spot

By SHELLEE NUNLEY
The Desert Sun

RANCHO MIRAGE — A hiding spot for such celebrities as Jamie Farr, Yul Brenner and Rod Serling, the White Sun Guest Ranch began on a smaller scale as a private ranch in the early 1920s.

Known then as the Eleven Mile Ranch — because it was 11 miles from Palm Springs — the site became a school for asthmatic children operated by Dr. Earl Tarr.

In 1946, Jack Dengler and his wife, Helen, bought the ranch — 10 acres and "a bunch of old houses" — for $25,000.

Under the Denglers' stewardship, the ranch grew to 60 acres with a nine-hole golf course, date palms, citrus and pasture. The ranch was eventually enlarged to include 72 rooms, a main lodge, ballroom, restaurant, four pools, six tennis courts and stables.

It became a hiding spot for celebrities, including Serling, Ginger Rogers, Norman Lear and Farr, said Kathy Mitchell, a Palm Desert resident who managed the ranch for 15 years.

"They could find rest and seclusion there. Nobody bothered them," Mitchell said.

Now residents of Del Rio, Texas, the Denglers have fond memories of their colorful clientele. Helen

Dengler recalled Brenner's habit of eating breakfast with the staff before his morning ride.

At night the guests would often coax Helen Dengler into playing accordion in the bar.

"It was a lot of work, but it was very stimulating. We had so many interesting people. Everybody was on a first-name basis," she said.

By 1980, however, the ranch's open vistas were gone and the land where guests used to ride had become Palm Desert.

They sold the ranch to a San Francisco firm which later re-

opened it as a gay resort called "The New Lost World Resort."

The New Lost World Resort lasted until 1988, when the doors were closed again.

An Agoura development company, Braemar, bought the property and plans to build 67 single-family homes on 18 acres of the original ranch site and another 88 houses on the other side of the Palm Valley Storm Channel, to be called Braemar White Sun Ranch.

Staff Writer Rose Wojnar contributed to this report.

File photo

AS IT WAS: The White Sun Guest Ranch clubhouse in 1990.

Rancho Mirage hotel fire

Site of fire — former White Sun Guest Ranch

Rancho Las Palmas Country Club

Monterey Ave.

Fred Waring Dr.

Joshua Rd.

Magnesia Falls Dr.

111

Palm Desert

Rancho Mirage

Bob Hope Dr.

SEAN McDADE/ The Desert Sun

RESORT LOST: The front of the White Sun Guest Ranch was a complete loss as the fire skipped from it to nearby trees and bushes,

destroying the entire area. Since the building was abandoned, officials could not give a dollar amount on the loss.

---

abandoned building, firefighters allowed the main, L-shaped clubhouse to burn but stopped the blaze from spreading to the guest rooms or adjacent neighborhoods, including Marriott's Rancho Las Palmas Country Club, he said.

Firefighters spent most of Monday afternoon and evening at the site on Joshua Road behind the country club, putting out the blaze and sifting for clues.

McConnell said the cause is under review, and investigators will consider arson.

Power, gas and water at the club were shut off, he said.

McConnell said wood samples will be sent to a crime lab to determine if a flammable liquid was used. He didn't know when results would be available.

McConnell said a handful of firefighters stayed at the scene, at one time called the New Lost World Resort, until late Monday, checking debris for hot spots.

Some area residents paid special attention to the blaze as they stood on a corner three blocks away.

"We wanted to make sure they got that guy out before the wind blew it in our backyard," Bonnie Williams said. "Everything is so dry this time of year."

Her friend, Lori Mullen, checked the wind, hoping the light breeze wouldn't shift west and send embers toward her neighborhood.

Firefighters also monitored the wind, McConnell said.

"My main, initial concern was that we would have a wind change

that would throw embers over to Rancho Las Palmas," he said.

One fire engine was placed in the country club just in case, McConnell said.

But the breeze blew to the east, carrying embers to an open field.

Firefighters also had to deal with a lack of water.

The first firefighters at the club found the closest hydrant more than one-half mile away, delaying their attack by minutes, fire officials said. No hydrants are on the property because of the resort's age, Clyde Chittenden, fire marshal for the Cove Communities, said.

In new housing developments, hydrants must be no farther than 400 feet apart, he said.

3. A different version of Southland Land and Realty Company's dream re-emerged full blown in 1946, with R. M. C. Fullenwider, who was secretary/manager of the Riverside County Fair's National Date Festival. An Arabian theme was adopted, inspired by the date palms' origin in Algeria. The festival included Hollywood set designers, choreographers and producers, a Queen Scheherazade and her Court contest, camel and ostrich races, and an Arabian Nights Musical Fantasy with colorful costumes and bazaars. That annual February event still takes place in Indio, California, eleven miles east of the ranch.

Chapter 3—How Many Bales of Hay?

Note to page 21

1. Jack Dengler's choice of the name WHITE SUN has stood the test of time. In the 1920s the first homesteader named the property, The Eleven Mile Ranch. In the 1930s Dr. Earl Tarr changed it to Hacienda de la Sanidad. For the next four decades it was known as WHITE SUN. It was changed briefly in the 1980s to Lost World Resort, but by the turn of the 21st Century, it was renamed White Sun Estates.

Chapter 4—SITA Reunions

Note to page 35

1. In her book TRAVELS WITH BICYCLE AND ACCORDION, published in 1997, (second edition 1999) the author provides a history of SITA (Students International Travel Association).

Chapter 5—The Ever Changing Oasis

Notes to pages 57, 75–76

1.   WHITE SUN

If I could paint, I would not paint the sun
In white—or make the sky by night dark blue;

Or do the grapefruit in a shiny green,
It's golden treasures peeking out between—
Not at White Sun.

I would not harmonize the tamarisk grays
As frequently I see them where I sit
Beside it, listening to the song of birds.
Paint harmonies are no conforming thirds—
Not at White Sun.

But I would add heart-filling reds
For human warmth; the richer yellows too.
Subtly I'd paint in Helen and her crew—
Their warmth of woman's hospitality—
Here at White Sun.

And somehow on the white-washed walls,
The well-kept flag-stoned walks, the hearthside browns
The somber colors of the hills that frown;
Diaphanous magentas I'd lay over—
Here at White Sun.

For colors are not "colors-in-a-tube."
Oh no! They need to breathe and come alive.
They need to feed the heart so they too thrive
From life itself, as well they seem to do—
Here at White Sun.

     —Milton Heimlich, White Sunner

2. The giant tamarisk tree that sheltered the ranch patio (pictured at the beginning of Chapter 5) was chopped down by developers on September 4, 1998, the same day Jack Dengler died at his home in Del Rio, Texas.

Relatives of this tamarisk tree, more commonly known as salt cedar, were introduced in the United States, as an ornamental, sometime in the 1850s. A native of Eurasia, it lives in bushy and grass covered semi-deserts, where it thrives on the shores of the Caspian Sea, across central Asia to northwestern China. Its five petal flowers are pink to white.

273

Soon after its introduction in the U.S., it became a serious threat along streams, canals, and reservoirs in the West. Now dominant in the Colorado River basin below 2,000 feet, it spreads rapidly via wind-dispersed seeds, which germinate in less than 24 hours! Its phenomenal reproductive output, great drought and flood tolerance have enabled it to invade watercourses and wetland habitats, taking over millions of acres throughout the Southwest. It thrives in very saline, nutrient-poor soil, spreading rapidly not only by seed, but by root, trunk, and branch sprouts.

At White Sun, tamarisk windbreaks greatly reduced sandblow, just as they protected Coachella Valley date and citrus orchards. The Southern Pacific Railroad was sheltered along its desert tracks by a tunnel of tamarisks. The trees also provided an abundant source of winter firewood for us at the ranch.

3. The Perry Mason television episode, filmed at White Sun during the 1950s, was one of many films produced in the desert, a favorite locale for Hollywood film-makers, and "playground of the stars."

Chapter 8—Tahiti's Madame Bobbie

Note to page 113

1. Our SITA agent in Tahiti, Madame Bobbie, provided us with the following instructions for a Tahitian Tamaraa:

MENU

Raw Fish could be prepared, if you could get hold of tuna, frozen when very fresh. We have to do it now in Tahiti, as we can no longer get enough fresh fish in Moorea for our large parties. Frozen tuna does very well, and you could try it now on a small scale, to see the results.

Depending on what you get, you could prepare the fish in two different ways:

Fish Salad: Skin the fish, take out the bones and cut out the dark meat, using only the white meat. Cut the fish in small pieces, thick as a finger and half as long. Salt, and pour on some vinegar,

274

stirring several times and checking to see that the vinegar soaks well into the fish. Better to work this with the hands for large quantities.

After soaking two hours, pour out the juice, keeping some of it in a bowl. Season with oil, pepper, and seasoning to taste. It is possible that some more salt, or some more vinegar juice should be added. When it is pleasant to the taste, add shredded carrots, tomatoes, cucumbers, green peppers, and decorate with hard-boiled eggs cut in small pieces.

(This recipe is useful in places where you can't get coconuts to prepare coconut milk.)

Raw Fish, as served in a Tamaraa in Tahiti: prepare the fish in the same way and let it soak in lime juice. The fish must be almost covered with lime juice. Turn several times with the hands. After two hours remove the pieces of fish from the lime juice, squeezing them strongly between the hands. Make a sauce with coconut milk which you have poured slowly over some sweet mustard and ketchup. Pour this sauce over the raw fish (this should not be done too long before the meal is served, approximately half an hour.) Check the taste and add salt or tomato ketchup. Add boiled eggs cut in small pieces and sweet cucumbers cut in squares.

If you can find coconuts which still have their water inside, they will do all right. Grate the coconut, pour a little hot water over it (a full coffee cup over each nut) and squeeze. Should you not be able to find coconuts, (at AIMEO, my hotel on Moorea, we need about 150 coconuts for a tamaraa, for 100 persons), for raw fish fafa you could try with fresh cream. It's not quite as good as coconut milk, but it works. I have tried it in France and Crista has too.

I wouldn't wonder but what you could make quite good fafa (the vegetable) with simple spinach, if only you can get the coconut milk. Cook the spinach two minutes in boiling water, then let it drain. Cut onion and garlic in small pieces, much more onion than garlic, of course. Cut small squares of raw ham, fry them with the

275

onions and garlic, add the spinach, one glass of cognac for 100 persons, salt, pepper, and approximately three large cups of coconut milk. Bake in a sealed or well covered pan in any oven. The steam must be kept in.

Roasted Suckling Pig, the piece de resistance (in Tahiti buried in the earth over hot stones) is easily done in any oven: to prepare the pig, pound about 10 pieces of garlic with salt, for each suckling pig, until it makes a paste. Rub the pig first with soy sauce, then with the salt and garlic. Bake the pig until well browned. Serve with boiled sweet potatoes, boiled bananas and baked pineapple slices, with which you decorate the pig. The sweet potatoes can be boiled first, then cut in thick slices, put in a pan, greased with butter and browned lightly in the oven. Canned pineapple can be used, better if they simmer a while in the pig's juices and then browned on the back of the pig.

You will have to be careful when choosing the bananas. There is a long, curved banana which is very good to eat raw, but does not cook well. You should use a straight, short banana, which we call rio. It boils well and makes good poi.

Poi (dessert): you should have pia, arrowroot starch. If you can get the bananas I recommend, you should have no difficulty making poi. You could also serve coconut ice cream, made with the milk of the coconut, and decorated with grated coconut when served.

With a good rum punch before, during and after, you should have no trouble achieving success!

Rum Punch: mix different blends, Martinique, Bourbon, Cuba. For 100 people, 12 hours before the party, add to the rum (two Planters Punch per person): 12 peeled bananas. Dissolve sugar, ¼ teaspoon per glass in a small amount of water, add pineapple juice to taste and let stand. Before serving, pound the peel of 4 green limes with some sugar, put the whole thing in the punch. Add lime juice to taste. Figure a half teaspoon of lime juice per glass. Filter and serve on shaved ice, with a long piece of fresh pineapple.

As decorations for the table, you could have baskets of pineapple, bananas, oranges, limes, and coconuts, if papayas are not to be found. Also pieces of watermelon.

At the ranch you could easily reproduce the table decoration we have at AIMEO. It consists of a centerpiece cut in a banana trunk, crowned with the top green part of the pineapple, and surrounded with flowers strung on a coconut leaf rib, and pieces of fruit stuck on picks. I believe you can find a soft material in which to cut the centerpiece, use wire to string the flowers and cocktail sticks for the fruit.

Decoration will not be difficult for you at the ranch with palm trees growing everywhere, and citrus plants. Tahitians use banana trees as decoration in corners and along columns, and in between the leaves garlands of flowers. If no greenery is available, garlands could be made of paper to give the general impression.

Try your hand at the recipes. I am very happy if you are happy.

With love,
Jeanne

Chapter 10—Music Round-Up

Notes to pages 147 and 151

1. For White Sun's 25th Anniversary, Lloyd and Priscilla Dunn contributed the following verses:

ODE TO WHITE SUN
(Sung to the melody of Gilbert & Sullivan's Admiral's Song)

We are Lloyd and Priscilla Dunn,
We are old, old timers at the old White Sun.
We came when the place was very small,
There was hardly any room for the guests at all.

Chorus

There was hardly any room for the guests you see,
For the place was filled with Jack and Helen's family.

There was lots to do and not many hands,
And Helen served dinner out of old bean cans.
She worked very late without any rests,
While Jack was playing banjo for the female guests.

 Chorus

While Jack was playing banjo for the female guests.

His rep-utation spread internationally
From north of San Francisco to the Salton Sea.

 Chorus

His rep-utation spread inter-nationally
From Casa Blanca to the Zuider Zee.

Then the travel agency took Jack afar,
He was always in Pretoria or Zanzibar,
Leaving Helen/ without a man,
And all she had to squeeze was her accordian.

 Chorus

And all she had to squeeze was her accordian. (Poor girl)

She squeezed and she squeezed and she said, "Thank God"
That Papa sent me studying to Juilliard.

 Chorus

She squeezed and she squeezed and she said, "Thank God"
That Papa sent me studying to Juilliard.

Yes Helen waited patiently,
For Ulysses to come home to his Penelope.
There never was any marital erosion
As they added to the population explosion.

Chorus

Yes they added to the population explosion.

Yes a large family at the White Sun rose,
But how they found the time to do it, no one knows.

Then Jack began to lend a hand.
He bought a bulldozer and he pushed some sand.
He built a golf course right out of his head,
And those who tried to play it wish that he was dead.

Chorus

And those who tried to play it wish that he were dead.

For when they try to drive a green
Their comments are derogatory and obscene.

Now it's 25 years and we still come back,
To Grandma Helen and Grandpa Jack.
We watch all the changes, one by one,
But the spirit stays the same at the old White Sun.

Chorus

Yes the spirit stays the same at the old White Sun.

With friendly guests how the time does pass,
Whether playing paddle tennis or sitting on the grass.

And some of us now are as rich as Midas,
But we can't play tennis 'cause we got arthritis.
For serving the ball pulls your arm too far,
But we still can bend an elbow at the White Sun Bar.

Chorus

They still can bend an elbow at the White Sun Bar.

They bend that elbow so frequently,
It is far more limber than their shoulder or knee.

279

While our feelings tonight are deeply moved,
There is one thing here they have never improved.
When you go to bed late, and you're feeling swell,
Early in the morning there's the breakfast bell.

Chorus

Early in the morning there's the breakfast bell.

Your eyes are red and your head begins to swell
To the clang, clang, clang of the breakfast bell.

You need that breakfast like a hole in the head,
But the bell sounds urgent, so you stumble out of bed.
No time for make-up or the old toothbrush,
You pull on your pants and you rush, rush, rush!

Chorus

You pull on your pants and you rush, rush, rush!

With a wobbly gait and a soul full of hate,
You stagger on in, but they say, "Too late!"
Perhaps some day the guests will rebel,
And put a big crack in that breakfast bell!

Chorus

They'll put a big crack in that breakfast bell!

(Slower)

Now as we sing for you tonight,
Sweet memories are reflected in the firelight.
In a world that is weary with doubt and fear,
We know that peace and happiness await us here.

Chorus

We know that peace and happiness await us here.

(Then, as The Finale, and sung to the tune of

280

The Wanderer's Song)

In the shade I lie and ponder,
While the White Sun waits out yonder.
My one wish is that I,
May visit White Sun till I die.

I have sought valleys enchanted,
I have sailed seas to far horizons.
But heat, cold, wind, drought or rain,
Our love for White Sun will remain.

(Repeat, full harmony and octaves.)

Heat, cold, wind, drought or rain,
Our love for White Sun will remain.

For a longer look into Lloyd Dunn's life, read his autobiography, ON THE FLIP SIDE.

2. "There Is A Better Way—Find It!" is the byline of Ed Burton's weekly column in THE WILLITS NEWS, and could well be his motto for life. Inventor and long-time White Sunner from Willits, California, Ed currently holds 23 U.S. patents and 2 from abroad. Although he and his wife Hattie, daughters Marjorie and Barbara, and Bruce had all been regulars at the ranch since the 1950s, I had never heard about Ed's Microphor Company until the 1970s. That was something I learned driving to Montana, when I stopped at a highway roadside rest area, and discovered his Microphor toilets installed there.

Ed began working with redwood bark in sewage treatment back in 1957. This led to the formation of Microphor, Inc. in 1963. With a jet flush using the barest minimum of water, Microphor, today is the leading worldwide manufacturer of toilets and treatment systems for boats, trains, and other extreme and remote locations.

Before selling Microphor in 1980, Ed began studying smoke control, resulting in the development of the Kleensmoke Burner, now known as the Inverse Pile Burner, for the destruction of unlogged wood waste. Another of his projects is Wind-Eco and Marsh Forest Systems, for treating sewage effluent, while creating an enhanced wildlife habitat and timber crop.

Ed Burton enhanced our White Sun habitat with many hilarious logger ballads (a favorite—ONCE I HEARD A CHICKEN SNEEZE) while playing the one-stringed guitar that hung on the bar wall.

Chapter 11—Jan Rouse

Note to page 183

1. Regarding Jan Rouse's sailing cruise with the Vern Kirkby's, she wrote us on June 9, 2001:

"We were on their ketch THE BLACK DOG, a 36 footer, sailing down from Vancouver through the San Juan Islands. ... We had a fabulous adventure together.

"I can thank White Sun for the Kirkbys. ... Actually White Sun was a catalyst and launching ground for many special new friendships, for many people. That's why so many persons became addicted to White Sun,— they knew they'd meet other enchanting people and families.

"All the Denglers gave the world a great gift through sharing their warm and joyful White Sun Ranch with so many of us!"

Chapter 14—Dorothy Neumann

Note to page 208

1. South African Josef Marais' hauntingly beautiful WANDERER'S SONG became SITA's and White Sun's theme song over half a century ago. Balladeer Josef was happy to grant us permission to reproduce the music.

JOSEF
MARAIS

Courtesy
National
Concert &
Artist Corp.

SING THE WANDERER!

Fifteen years ago SITA's theme song was adopted by a cycle group who were enroute to Stratford-on-Avon. Already a favorite of E-12A'49's leader, Helen Dengler, Josef Marais' hauntingly beautiful WANDERER'S SONG is now sung by SITA groups everywhere and has also become White Sun Guest Ranch's theme song. Balladeer Josef Marais' who was born in South Africa, writes us as follows:

"You ask how I came to write the WANDERER'S SONG. It was during the run on the NBC network of my radio program AFRICAN TREK, 1946 that I needed a nice lazy song which would put into music the inner urge of most people to travel to distant lands—easy-like with leisure and a keen appetite to taste the flavor of other countries. The WANDERER'S SONG was born and sung on one of these radio programs, as a group of us rode on horseback across the African Veld. It isn't a great work of art, and yet, even great works have been produced by great artists like Michelangelo to a definite assignment! The WANDERER'S SONG since that time has been sung in many a concert by Miranda and yours truly, and by many a group of people who love the open sky . . . Now you tell me of your people singing it in distant lands like Hawaii, Tahiti, Japan and of course Miranda and I are delighted to know the song has epitomized the yearning of so many people: we hope it will continue to be sung for many a year to come!

Sincerely yours,

Josef Marais."

Words and Music by Josef Marais

NOTE: Lower voice carries melody.

"THE WANDERER'S SONG"
Used by Permission — All Rights Reserved

1. In the shade, I lie and ponder, as the sun's rays beat out yonder
2. I will seek valleys en- chanted, I will find lakes that are haunted.

My one wish is that I — may wander the world 'til I die.
Heat, cold, wind, drought or rain, a wanderer, I will re- main.

The Desert's Most Sheltered, Centrally Situated Community

RANCHO MIRAGE

Located in the geographic center of the Coachella Valley, ten miles from Palm Springs to the northwest and Indio to the southeast, Rancho Mirage lies in a sheltered cove of the Santa Rosa Mountains, at the junction of two highways, which intersect the desert and the mountains. Every attraction of this sunshine wonderland is quickly accessible: open desert, dramatic canyons, the greatest golfing area in the world. ■ The community rises above the surrounding valley at an elevation of 246 feet. Dry, clear air and low humidity; pure, deep well water . . . and plenty of it . . . casual living at its unhurried, uncrowded best . . . Rancho Mirage offers ideal living conditions. ■ The first man to develop land in Rancho Mirage was R. P. ("Bert") Davie, an ardent promoter from Michigan. "I'm gonna buy this country", he commented after seeing the flourishing date groves at nearby Wonder Palms. With his mules and a fresno he dug out Rio Del Sol and subdivided his acreage, known as "Little Santa Monica". By 1928 Davie was ready to plant his first date shoots, now grown tall and proud among the many beautiful ranches along Rio Del Sol. ■ The first map of Rancho Mirage was filed October 23, 1924, and the name was dreamed up by a Los Angeles realtor, Lawrence Macomber, the creator of Emerald Bay. Macomber needed a salesman with imagination and ingenuity and acquired the services of a Canadian named Don Cameron in 1934. The airpark came in 1945, world famous Thunderbird Country Club in 1946. The row of mailboxes Cameron erected on the Veldt in 1937 grew to a post office in 1951, and by 1962 the pattern of growth in Rancho Mirage was a concrete $80,000 first class post office! ■ Three shopping cen-

LUCILLE BALL
Honorary Mayor

(Courtesy Desilu Productions Inc.)

ters, cosmopolitan restaurants, luxury hotels, motels and a world famous guest ranch admirably cater to the whims of tourist and resident alike. Thriving ranches on Rio Del Sol produce dates, citrus and grapes. Alert citizens are planning the orderly growth of Rancho Mirage through their Community Association, the Rancho Mirage Chamber of Commerce and the Women's Club. ■ Two private schools take care of pre-school children and the first eight grades. Public school busses from both Palm Springs and Indio school districts service Rancho Mirage and an elementary school is in the planning stage. In 1962 the College of the Desert, a campus of the University of California, opened its doors on the threshold of Rancho Mirage, serving students from the entire Coachella Valley and a growing number from out-of-state. ■ Recreation in bewildering variety is close at hand: golf, swimming, tennis, riding, hiking in the wilderness of Magnesia Falls Canyon, home of the Rocky Mountain Bighorn Sheep. ■ A residential community of beautiful homes, Rancho Mirage has long been known as "Palm Springs' favorite suburb". Be it the glamorous Thunderbird Country Club, the bucolic charm of Clancy Lane or a cool adobe on the Veldt, a warm welcome awaits you in this friendly desert community. ■ Rancho Mirage's civic pride is evident in its "Memory Lane", a row of trees, with the donors' names inscribed on a stone-mounted plaque, at the handsome new post office. Eight Desert Beautiful awards have been presented to business and professional men, who have contributed to the beautification of the Coachella Valley, in Rancho Mirage. A drive to satisfy future recreation needs is now underway to secure a park in Magnesia Falls Canyon.

"Build Your Future in Rancho Mirage"

Notes to pages 248, 252, and 255

1. Lolomi Lodge and the Trailfinders School property became "The James San Jacinto Mountain Reserve," part of the University of California's Natural Reserve System, as reported in DPC's 35th Anniversary Report.

2. After joining the Rancho Mirage Chamber of Commerce, among other duties, Helen produced a 1965 brochure for the Chamber.

3. During the 1960s my neighbor Randall Henderson personified the desert for me, and thousands of others who read his DESERT MAGAZINE. Randall worked as a sports reporter for the LOS ANGELES TIMES, while a student at the University of California. His editor, Harry Carr advised him to "... leave this city rat race to work for a small newspaper."

Henderson did so, starting out as an apprentice printer on the weekly POST, in Parker, Arizona, and then on THE HERALD, in Blythe, California. Next he edited and published his own paper, in Calexico on the California-Mexico border until 1933, when he moved on to El Centro and opened a printing shop.

Exploring the desert by foot and by horseback, he became intimately acquainted with its canyons, hidden oases, flora and fauna. One day by a campfire in the Santa Rosa Mountains, Randall and Wilson McKinney, a newspaper associate, came up with the idea for DESERT MAGAZINE. The first issue was printed on November 1, 1937.

Henderson had been a pilot in World War I and re-enlisted in World War II, asking for an assignment in Africa. While in Africa he decided to move his magazine to Palm Desert, already a meeting place for artists, scientists and writers. The handsome DESERT MAGAZINE building was completed in 1948. Henderson continued as DESERT's Publisher until 1962. Staunch desert advocate, he continued writing articles to educate the public, encouraging others to fight for wilderness and desert protection. Here is one of his stories:

WHERE WILD PALMS GROW
by Randall Henderson

DESERT MAGAZINE, March 1965

There are nine species of trees indigenous to the Southern California desert, and if I were asked to name the one which I regard as the most ornate, I would reply without hesitation: the wild palm, Washingtonia filifera.

My acquaintance with this stately tree growing in its native habitat, was in 1921. My prospector friend, Gus Lederer, had invited me to visit his little cabin at Corn Springs in the Chuckawalla Mountains. Following his directions, I took a rock road from the floor of Chuckawalla Valley up a canyon where he and his burros made their home.

Rounding a bend in the canyon, immediately in front of me, was a picture one would never expect to find in an arid desert—a majestic group of palm trees encircling a spring of flowing water. Later I counted 82 trees ranging in height from 30 to 50 feet, green fronds at their crowns, and skirts of dead fronds reaching almost to the ground. Obviously this oasis had once been the camping ground of prehistoric desert tribesmen, for the rocks surrounding the spring were adorned with the petroglyphic art of Indians, and there were deep mortar holes in some of the boulders.

Since then, the exploration of desert canyons in quest of wild palm groups has been a hobby, and during the intervening years I have logged 87 separate oases in the canyons and foothills of Riverside, San Bernardino, San Diego and Imperial counties. My estimate is that there are at least 11,000 native palms on the Southern California Desert, approximately half of them in Riverside county.

Two other palm canyons in this general area should be mentioned. Bear Creek palms are reached by a fine 3-mile trail, which climbs the southern slope of La Quinta, and Magnesia Falls Canyon, with a pretty little ampitheater at its entrance, the pride of Rancho Mirage, where residents are making a valiant effort to have it set aside as a county park.

Whence came these palms in an arid land, for abundant water is necessary for their growth and health? No one knows the answer to this question. But it is generally believed they are the descendants of a fringe of wild palms which grew along the shoreline of the Gulf of California, which long ago covered the entire below sea-level basin now known as Imperial and Coachella valleys. Occasional survivors in their original habitat may be seen along the old shoreline on the north side of Coachella valley and in the Borrego Badlands.

But this theory does not explain the greater number of palms growing in the canyons up to 3200 feet. Perhaps prehistoric Indians, who ground and used the seeds for food, carried them up creekbeds to their present habitat. My own conclusion—and it is only a theory—is that the lowly coyote deserves much of the credit for transporting the seeds into the canyons where the palms now grow. The coyotes eat the fruit, but digest only the sweet skin that covers the seed. During many years of traversing these canyons I have frequently observed undigested seeds of the Washingtonia in the dung of coyotes along the creekbeds. This has been true both on the California desert and in Baja, California, where palm canyons are found on much of the length of the peninsula.

True, the coyote is a chicken thief and a camp robber—but, he also has his virtues. Unwittingly, of course, but nevertheless I believe it is true that Don Coyote, more than any other agent brought the majestic wild palm to the canyons of our desert land.

Bibliography

Bennett, Melba: STORY OF DEEP WELL, Palm Springs, California, Palm Springs VILLAGER 1948

Burke, Tony: PALM SPRINGS WHY I LOVE YOU, Palm Desert. California, Palmesa, Inc. 1978

Chase, J. Smeaton: CALIFORNIA DESERT TRAILS, Boston & New York. Houghton Mifflin Co., 1919

Cornett, James W.: DESERT PALM OASIS, Santa Barbara, California, Companion Press, for the Palm Springs Desert Museum 1989

Dengler, John C. Jr: THE WORLD WAS MY BACKYARD, Unpublished autobiography, Del Rio, Texas 1992

Harrison, Hal H.: FIELD GUIDE TO WESTERN BIRDS' NESTS, Boston Ma., Houghton Mifflin Co. 1979

Havert, Bill: RESOLVING THE PENINSULAR BIGHORN SHEEP ISSUE, Temecula, California, Coachella Valley Mountains Conservancy, Dec. 23, 1998

James, Harry: CAUTION; SCIENTISTS AT WORK, Palm Desert, California, DESERT MAGAZINE, March 1964 Issue

Jennings, Bill & Irwin P. Ting: Special photographic section by Ansel Adams: DEEP CANYON, A DESERT WILDERNESS FOR SCIENCE, Riverside, California, Philip L. Boyd Deep Canyon Research Center, University of California at Riverside 1976

Pepper, Jack: RANDALL HENDERSON, Palm Desert, Ca. DESERT MAGAZINE March 1964 Issue

Rancho Mirage Cultural Commission: A LOOK BACK IN TIME, City of Rancho Mirage, 1993 and 1997

Richards, Elizabeth: A LOOK INTO PALM SPRINGS' PAST, Palm Springs, Ca., Santa Fe Federal Savings & Loan Assn. 1961

Shirley, Dennis: THE POLITICS OF PROGRESSIVE EDUCATION— The Odenwaldschule in Nazi Germany, Harvard University Press, Cambridge, Massachusetts, London England 1992

SITAGRAM News letter: SITA World Travel, Inc., Rancho Mirage, Ca., 1949 to 1969 Issues

Tevis, Yvonne Pacheco: THE COACHELLA VALLEY PRESERVE, San Bernardino, Ca., The Borgo Press, 1995

Wheat, Frank: CALIFORNIA MIRACLE, THE FIRST FOR DESERT PARKS & WILDERNESS, San Diego, California, Sunbelt Publications 1999

WHITE SUN ROUND-UP Newsletter: Rancho Mirage, Ca., SITA Print Shop, 1951 to 1979 Issues

Index

294

Jack takes Helen for a ride in the Taiwan pedicab, a gift from Robert Chu in SITA's Taipei office.

November 1963
True Slocum Photo

About the Author

Born in Madison, Wisconsin, Helen Dykema Dengler studied music abroad, at the Diller Quaile and Juilliard Schools of Music in New York City, graduated from Barnard College, and studied advanced composition with Arnold Schönberg at the University of California at Los Angeles.

From 1934 to 1959 she helped her husband, Jack Dengler, build SITA (Students' International Travel Association) into a world-wide tour operator, while conducting bicycle tours, editing the SITAGRAM, and working as SITA's public relations director. During the fifties, she managed Jack's White Sun Guest Ranch in Rancho Mirage, California, which became SITA's world headquarters.

The author's passions include: organic gardening, Bach, Fauré, chocolate labrador retrievers, photography, and Mah Jongg. She spends winters on the Mexican border in the West Texas city of Del Rio, and summers close to the Canadian border in Big Arm, Montana.

The Denglers have six children and five grandchildren.